Eco-Refurbishment
A guide to saving and producing energy in the home

Other Architectural Press books by the author

Architecture in a Climate of Change:
A Guide to Sustainable Design
(2001)

Sustainability at the Cutting Edge:
Emerging Technologies for Low Energy Buildings
(2002)

Eco-Refurbishment

A guide to saving and producing energy in the home

Peter F. Smith

AMSTERDAM • BOSTON • HEIDELBERG • LONDON • NEW YORK • OXFORD
PARIS • SAN DIEGO • SAN FRANCISCO • SINGAPORE • SYDNEY • TOKYO

Architectural Press is an imprint of Elsevier

Architectural
Press

Architectural Press
An imprint of Elsevier
Linacre House, Jordan Hill, Oxford OX2 8DP
200 Wheeler Road, Burlington, MA 01803

First published 2004

British Library Cataloguing in Publication Data
A catalogue record for this book is available from the British Library

Library of Congress Cataloguing in Publication Data
A catalogue record for this book is available from the Library of Congress

ISBN 0 7506 5973 4

For information on all Architectural Press publications
visit our website at www.architecturalpress.com

Composition by Genesis Typesetting Ltd, Rochester, Kent
Printed and bound by Martins the Printers, Berwick upon Tweed

Contents

CONTENTS

Foreword

I believe that today we are living in a land of no tomorrow! I say *no tomorrow*, because we dare not look there, at tomorrow, at our future. For how can we, a decent society who so value human rights and so love our children whose needs and wellbeing we so dearly care for; how can we reconcile these values with lifestyles that will inevitably produce the disastrous future that will be our legacy to our children, and children's children? Think about it. We are the first generation to knowingly 'hand' the planet to our descendants in a worse condition than we inherited it – and the key word here is *knowingly*. There is no excuse: we know. If you don't already know then from here on you are on formal notice: you know now, so remember . . . and spread the word. Fast!

The truth is, of course, that we intend none of these things, but we have become, quite unwittingly, part of a growing world order that is *unsustainable*.

My grandparents grew up in Herefordshire in the UK in the early 1900s. For them, travel was rare, and food was almost entirely locally produced. Today, the average meal on a UK plate will have travelled 2500 miles. Fruit and vegetables brought by air to our land out of season; exotic sea foods from far away waters, and indeed our own livestock transported across Europe for slaughter in far off places. Must we live like this? The so-called 'developed world' has *progressed*, in just three hundred years, from economies based on sail and hay, to sail and coal, to coal and oil, and now in some cases, to oil and gas. Can we find a safer fuel source – one which is both renewable and which does not produce such environmentally damaging by-products? Does a hydrogen based economy offer any hope?

Alarmingly, our failing is in almost everything we do: the clothes we wear, the furniture we buy, the consumer durables that we rely upon. Even our shoes are assembled with a combination of glues and rubbers that render them virtually impossible to recycle. For an ever increasing proportion of our needs we use 'bio-nutrients' and 'techno-nutrients' that are not recyclable – not renewable. Accordingly we are now breaking all the rules which have successfully sustained life on this planet for millions of years and we are breaking those rules big-time and fast.

But you at least care. Perhaps you have adopted good shopping policies through which you, as a *consumer*, encourage ethical and ecologically responsible manufacturing and retailing policies. Either way, you want to learn more about how your own home can be made more sustainable. Otherwise, why would you have bought this book?

Maybe you live in a town or a city. Most of us now do and indeed sometime around the turn of the 21st century the balance of living, globally, switched in favour of urbanization. From here on, more than 50 per cent of the world's population will live in towns and cities. As such, their reliance on public utilities will be ever greater and their relationship with, and understanding of, the land and ecological systems that support our lives will become evermore tenuous. As an example, the survival of London today in terms of food supply and waste 'absorption' (as far as that is possible in the context of the extensive use of synthetic materials) requires a land area some three times that of the UK – or put another way, a land area the size of Spain. Despite this extraordinary and alarming fact, the vast majority of Londoners have no concept of the demands that their city, or their collective lifestyles, place on the environment; of where their foods come from, how their waste is disposed of, or indeed of the enormous damage that their city does to our host planet.

It is not that Londoners are evil, or that they are any more irresponsible than town and city folk elsewhere. That, despite a collective intelligence and sophistication that we associate with urban living, the vast majority of them are 'disconnected' from any aware-ness or the kind of personal and collective sense of responsibility that is needed if we, as a society, are to avert disaster.

'The world's population increasingly live in cities where the air is unbreathable, the water is undrinkable, and the waste is unmanage-able' claim's Vasilles Sgoutas, a past president of the Union of International Architects. He knows that we cannot go on like this; that we have to live more responsible lifestyles and that once more, the 'cutting edge' of technology must find its way back into the construc-tion of our buildings, towns and cities. For without *intelligently* designed and *intelligent* architecture and urban facilities the human race is doomed. Buildings account for 50 per cent of the carbon emissions that are wreaking such havoc with our environment, trans-port for 30 per cent and agriculture and manufacturing for 20 per cent. Accordingly, it is critical that we get the emissions of buildings under control, but still we continue to produce new hospitals, offices, schools and houses – indeed every building type, with scant regard for the damage that our design strategies do in environmental terms.

So, it is quite clear that if we are to take hold of this problem, and to make major progress towards becoming ecologically respon-sible, we have to make major progress with our existing homes. And that's where this book comes in, providing a step by step guide for you, the homeowner who wants to live a more responsible lifestyle, and who wants to upgrade your home. This book will help you and your family to do just that.

Here you can learn about new forms of energy supply, about better and more efficient boilers, about more effective insulation, about how to treat incontinent buildings, about passive cooling, photo-voltaic cells, wind turbines, zero energy and emission strategies, domestic waste management, water conservation, the avoidance of toxic materials through 'informed' purchasing policies and much, much more. In easy to understand steps, Peter Smith takes you through a myriad of options from which you can select an ecologically responsible programme of alterations and 'facility management' policies to suit your own lifestyle, house and pocket.

As President of the RIBA, one of my repeated messages has been that *architecture belongs to architects no more than music to musicians*. That is a message that I have delivered time and time again in speeches, articles, radio and TV work, and it is a message that is particularly seminal to a public who want to use architecture responsibly. The RIBA charter calls on us as a profession to *advance architecture*, not, you will note, the interests of architects. This charter, granted back in 1837, has to my mind more relevance today than at any time in the history of the RIBA, and probably anytime in the history of architecture.

Let us consider some simple basics. In their earliest efforts to build, people's intentions were to protect themselves, and subsequently no doubt their possessions, from enemies and from inclement weather. Thereafter, they built to celebrate, to deify, to facilitate cultural, commercial and manufacturing activity, and to 'lift the spirit'. But none of these aspirations can be realized, or indeed have any sensible application, if our host environment will not support life. No life, no architecture . . . .

Which brings us to the awesome challenge that the human race now faces in tempering our lifestyles, and in particular the methods by which we support and service our needs, in order to sustain life on this planet. Many people will know of the 1987 Brundtland Commission, and its definition for sustainable development as being 'development that meets the needs of the present without compromising the need of future generations to meet their own needs'. And few will have difficulty in accepting that we must do our best to achieve that. Again, this book is designed to help you and your family in that endeavour.

When I decided, as President of the RIBA, that this book should be written, I could think of no-one better than my Vice President for Sustainability to do the job. Here, in this book that has been written specifically for the non-specialist, we have a tool that will enable us to do better where it matters most: in our homes.

Husbandry of our resources, and living within an ecologically sustainable lifestyle is our implicit duty to the children that we love so dearly, and to future generations as yet unborn. That duty starts at home. Your home, and my home . . . . And it starts today with this book in your hand . . . . Indeed, if we fail in this endeavour we fail in absolute terms for we will deny future generations the very basis for their survival. That would be the ultimate corruption and one that would be utterly corrosive of all that we hold precious in terms of social values.

That cannot be allowed to happen. Please read . . . . Please act . . . . Please lead by example, however small that may be . . . . And please persuade others to do the same.

Paul Hyett
Chairman of RyderHKS Architects and
President of the Royal Institute of British Architects
London
May 2003

Preface

First and foremost, this is a description of ways in which householders can reduce the consumption of energy in the home. As mentioned in the Government White Paper on Energy of February 2003, reducing the demand for energy, especially as produced by fossil fuels, is a high priority in the drive towards a sustainable future. Access to energy is a matter which will increasingly dominate our lives in the 21st century as fossil fuel reserves decline and prices rise. We will also come under growing pressure to reduce our emissions of the main greenhouse gas carbon dioxide caused mainly by the burning of fossil fuels coal, gas and oil.

Besides saving energy, there is an increasing climate of opinion in favour of renewable energy production. Meeting government targets for electricity from renewable sources will demand contributions not just from large wind farms, etc, but also from individuals who install photovoltaic cells on their roofs to reduce their reliance on imported electricity and contribute any surplus electricity to the grid.

However, the ecological agenda embraces other topics besides energy and the book will consider which materials, like paints and timber, are most environmentally acceptable. How to reduce waste is another aspect of sustainability as is the choice of the most energy-efficient appliances.

Finally, the book offers information on sources of expert advice concerning the installation of insulation and technologies for producing energy as well as advice on grants which may be available for both insulation measures and renewable electricity production. It must be borne in mind, however, that the grant regime changes at frequent intervals.

Peter F. Smith
March 2003

Acknowledgements

My thanks are due to Paul Hyett, who, as President of the Royal Institute of British Architects, suggested the idea for this book. I am also greatly indebted to Dr Randall Thomas of Max Fordham and Partners for his rigorous scrutiny of the draft text, resulting in numerous helpful suggestions and occasional corrections. I should also mention Nick White, who helped with the information about the Hockerton Project, Mary Wragg who supplied information about the solar collectors retrofitted to the roof of her home and David Hammond who readily gave me information about the heat pump installation in his home in Oxford.

Homes for the future from the past

Chapter One

Internationally, there is still a considerable short-fall in the take-up of energy saving measures in the home and the main reason is that energy is comparatively cheap. Replacing existing windows with double glazing has been popular, more for cosmetic than environmental reasons. So, why bother? Here are some of the reasons.

(1) At the time of writing oil prices are rising due to uncertainties about security of supplies from the Middle East, particularly centring on Iraq, which has the second largest reserves of oil in the region. At the same time, we are being continually reminded that reserves of oil and gas are finite. According to some analysts, the year 2003 will be the time when demand for oil outstrips supply, irrespective of a possible Middle East conflict. The more optimistic oil experts put the date at around 2005–7. For the UK the situation is exacerbated by the decline in North Sea oil production and the fact that gas reserves in this area will be exhausted by about 2016. Add to this the fact that most nuclear generators will have been decommissioned by roughly the same time and the problems are particularly acute. Price rises would therefore seem to be inevitable. If there is a widespread conflagration in the Middle East the price rise could be astronomic, triggering a world recession led by the USA. This is one very good reason why nations and individuals should minimize their reliance on fossil-based energy.

(2) As if this were not enough, global warming resulting mainly from the burning of fossil fuels is building up momentum. Almost each day there is evidence of climate changes and the situation is effectively irreversible. Even if human-induced emissions of greenhouse gases are levelled off immediately, the momentum in the system would continue to inflict climate damage for decades, even centuries to come. However, if things go on as they are, there is no immediate prospect of stabilizing those gases. The Johannesburg Summit of 2002 deliberately ignored the climate change issue, focusing on sustainable development. From the point of view of most governments and multinational corporations it is 'business as usual' which, according to the UN scientists is the worst case scenario (Intergovernmental Panel on Climate Change (IPCC) 2002). Without

going into detail, the main driver of climate change is the concentration of carbon dioxide (CO_2) in the atmosphere. This acts like a blanket, reflecting heat from the sun back to Earth which acts as a heat accumulator. Before the Industrial Revolution the CO_2 concentration was around 270 parts per million by volume (ppmv). Today it is approximately 380 ppmv (Washington Worldwatch Institute, 2003). The UN CO_2 abatement programme has an upper limit of 500 ppmv by 2050. It recognizes that at this level there will be considerable climate damage by flood, storm, ecological and social disruption. However, this target assumes that the world should have already adopted significant carbon reduction policies. There is still no sign that this will happen; the present shape of business globalization seems to guarantee that business as usual will prevail for the foreseeable future. If the big players prefer to ignore their responsibilities for the future welfare of the planet it is up to individuals to take up the challenge.

The effect of this could be dramatic. In the UK nearly 30 per cent of all CO_2 emissions are down to housing. This could quite reasonably be cut by half using the technology which will be outlined in this book. New homes are subject to reasonably stringent energy efficiency standards; it is the existing stock of homes which present the challenge, in particular those of private home owners and landlords.

(3) The pressure to upgrade our houses will soon come from the authorities. By 2005–6 regulations will come into force in the UK designed to speed up the home-buying process. A vendor will be required to provide a 'home condition report' based on a professional survey which will include an energy efficiency assessment (EEA) of the property. As energy prices rise, the EEA will increasingly become a deciding factor in a decision to purchase. At the same time a European Union directive 'Energy in Buildings' is likely to be incorporated into UK law by 2006. This states that houses over 10 years old must have a valid energy certificate at the time of sale.

(4) The upgrading of a property should immediately represent added capital value. At the same time, energy bills could be reduced by as much as 50 per cent per year. As prices rise this represents a valuable revenue gain. According to the government English House Condition Survey, over 85 per cent of pre-1965 housing has no wall insulation. It is no surprise then that up to 60 per cent of energy used in the home is expended on heating.

(5) What tends to be overlooked is the health impact of poorly insulated homes. Many householders endure inadequate room temperatures sometimes as low as 14°C which, for the elderly and infirm, is a major hazard. Of the 55 000 extra winter deaths which occurred in the UK in 1999–2000, up to half may be attributed to inadequate warmth. In addition, that winter there was a sharp rise in respiratory and cardiovascular illnesses.

The official standard for warmth in a living room is 21°C and in other rooms 18°C. About 25 per cent of homes in the UK achieve these levels. The minimum temperatures from the point of view of health are 18°C for living rooms and 16°C for other rooms. A government house condition survey for England found that, when the outside temperature fell to 4°C:

50 per cent of owner occupied homes
62 per cent of council homes
95 per cent of private rented apartments

all failed to reach the minimum standard.

Poorly insulated homes are not only cold, they are invariably damp. When warm air comes into contact with cold external walls it condenses into moisture. This, in turn, encourages mould growth which poses a serious health risk. This is a particular problem for the fuel poor. This is recognized by government: 'The principal effects of fuel poverty are health related, with children, the old, the sick and the disabled most at risk. Cold homes are thought to exacerbate existing illnesses such as asthma and reduce resistance to infections (*Fuel Poverty; The New HEES*, DETR 1999).

(6) What should also be factored in is the rise in comfort which can be experienced from investing in an insulation and draught-proofing strategy. Cold, uninsulated walls and single-glazed windows cause sharp thermal gradients which are often experienced as cold draughts. Condensation adds to this problem. This is particularly the case with uninsulated floors leading to the warm head–cold feet condition that is especially uncomfortable for people with poor circulation.

(7) Finally there is the matter of social responsibility. As mentioned above, it is becoming more evident that the welfare of the planet will increasingly depend on the actions of individuals and local communities. Upgrading one's home is not only a personal act of social responsibility, it may also stimulate the 'keeping up with the Jones' phenomenon. In addition there is the point that if a number of householders decide to upgrade simultaneously they may reap the financial benefits of bulk purchase through a large contract.

The house condition survey

A house behaves as an interactive system; all its components impinge on each other. For example, it is pointless achieving a high level of insulation in walls and roof if 40 per cent of space heating is lost through leakage. So, before undertaking a retrofit programme of insulation, etc., it is necessary to survey the property to gauge the extent of the work to be undertaken so that the procedures can be planned in the correct sequence. It is also wise to make an estimate of costs including a 10 per cent contingency sum. This will involve calculating areas, for example of the area of glazing which may need to be replaced. At this stage it is worth investigating the grants and 'green' mortgages that may be available from building societies. If routine maintenance is having to be undertaken, such as the replacement of roof tiles/slates, the cost of using it as an opportunity to insert or enhance insulation is a relatively small extra cost burden achieving a rapid payback time.

It is not always obvious to a householder whether or not the walls are solid or cavity construction. As regards the latter, if there are not records from previous owners, it will be necessary for the cavities to be inspected to see if insulation has been inserted. If there is such evidence, the next thing is to ensure that it is still viable up to eaves level. There is a tendency for fibrous insulants to settle over time.

It may be that there is some insulation in the loft space. However, it is most likely to be inadequate, on the basis that the loft is the most cost-effective zone in terms of the benefits of insulation.

Most older houses are draughty which can be a benefit in summer and an escape route for up to 40 per cent of heat in winter. Draught problems need to be identified and dealt with as the first priority. A really effective draught-proofing procedure must be linked to the need to maintain adequate ventilation. This will require specialist advice and will be covered in Chapter 5.

The opportunity should be taken to inspect the structural integrity of the property. Evidence of damp or cracks in walls must be attended to before installing insulation. Roof flashings should be inspected and replaced where necessary. At the same time, gutters and rainwater pipes should be in good condition. Damp walls are not only a cold bridge, they can also cause some insulation materials to lose efficiency.

Special attention should be paid to finishes, selecting paints and varnishes which are free of volatile organic compounds (VOCs).

Finally, it is important to ensure that all operatives hired to carry out retrofit work are validated by their respective trade or professional bodies and that all guarantees are robust and free of small print escape clauses. In certain instances permissions may have to be sought under Planning and Building Regulations legislation. In the UK under the 2002 Building Regulations Part L, certain aspects of retrofit work must comply with standards of insulation. This will be explained in detail in the text.

Priorities

At the outset it is worth considering which are the remedial measures which are cost effective in terms both of monetary cost and CO_2

emissions. There is little doubt which leads the field: loft insulation. Heat rises and a poorly insulated roof offers the perfect escape route. Also it is worth enquiring if grants are available at a particular time and the body to clarify this in the UK is the Energy Saving Trust. Its details are given below. At the time of writing the UK government is giving priority to persuading home owners to upgrade their properties, and money is often what makes the argument irresistible.

Straightforward draught-proofing can have a benefit out of all proportion to its cost. However, if the draught sealing has been carried out really effectively, it may be necessary to provide fan-assisted ventilation which can also recover heat from the warm expelled from the house. The power consumed is no more than a couple of average light bulbs.

Most post-1930 homes have cavity walls and still the majority in the UK do not have the benefit of cavity-fill insulation. The benefits of rectifying this deficiency can be felt immediately in increased comfort, as well as longer term in lower energy bills. Grants may be available. Refer to www.est.org.uk

Many central heating systems are well below current best practice. Upgrading the system starting with thermostatic valves fitted to radiators which set the temperature at a level which is appropriate to a room. For example, the radiator in an entrance hall does not need to emit heat at the same temperature as in the living room. The next move is to replace the boiler with a condensing version, an operation which might also attract a government subsidy.

Appliances and white goods are often major energy drains, especially fridges and freezers. When these come to be replaced it is vital that the most energy efficient products are selected. The additional cost of a highly energy efficient item could soon be recovered in lower running costs.

Double glazing has gained a hold on the housing sector, not least because of the assertive marketing tactics of some double glazing companies. In part, this is because it is perceived as a fashion accessory to a home. It certainly improves comfort by reducing the temperature drop within two or three feet of a window which is usually experienced as a draught. In terms of energy saving, depending on the area of glazing involved, the pay-back time can be quite long. Building regulations now require high performance double glazing which uses Low-E (low emissivity) glass.

Cold feet is a national malaise in the UK because floors are also a major heat drain. Inserting insulation into floors can be relatively cheap and easy if there is access to the underside of the floor. If not, there is probably no alternative to raising the floor boards.

Next in the hierarchy of cost comes insulating solid masonry walls. Insulating the inside face of external walls is the cheaper option, but is does involve reducing the floorspace, as well as relocating power sockets and light switches. However, the really significant results are achieved with external insulation or overcladding. Big results incur fairly dramatic costs, but most of these may be recovered in the increased capital value of a highly energy efficient overclad property, remembering the incoming regulations concerning an energy report as part of the seller's pack.

At the time of writing (January 2003) the UK government has announced a subsidy scheme aimed at home owners to encourage the installation of renewable energy systems like photovoltaic cells (PVs). Grants may make home energy production a viable proposition. In Europe, it will almost certainly be much more cost effective when the energy market is liberalized under EU regulations later in the decade.

In one or two cases indicative costs are given as a rough guide. In times of economic volatility it is hazardous to indicate prices. Wherever possible contact names, web sites, e-mail addresses and telephone numbers are given within the text.

Insulation options

Chapter Two

Warmth is a valuable commodity and it will seek every possible means to escape from our homes. Walls, roofs, floors, chimneys and windows are all escape routes, and in most homes escape is easy. The answer is to wrap the home in a thermal blanket which involves

- insulation; and
- draught sealing.

Space heating usually makes the greatest demand on energy. The procedures described below could reduce energy bills by up to 50 per cent and more in the most substandard properties. Starting with insulation, it is necessary to outline the range of insulants currently available and to summarize their characteristics. When we come to consider the elements of a house in detail, there will be further advice regarding the insulants appropriate to a particular situation since it is important to know that some insulants carry risks.

The range of options

There are numerous alternatives when it comes to choosing insulation materials. They differ in thermal efficiency and certain important properties, such as resistance to fire and avoidance of ozone-depleting chemicals. Some also lose much of their insulating efficiency if affected by moisture. So, at the outset it is advisable to understand something about the most readily available insulants. The thermal efficiency of an insulant is denoted by its thermal conductivity termed Lambda value measured in W/mK. The thermal conductivity of a material 'is the amount of heat transfer per unit of thickness for a given temperature difference' (Thomas, 1996: 10). Technically it is a measure of the rate of heat conduction through 1 m^3 of a material with a 1°C temperature difference across the two opposite faces. The lower the value the more efficient the material.

It is important to select insulants which have zero ozone-depleting potential (ZODP). There are three main categories of insulation material.

- Inorganic, mineral based
- Organic synthetic, derived from oil
- Natural organic, derived from animals and plants.

Mineral-based insulants come in two forms, fibre or cellular structure.

Fibre

Rock wool
Produced by melting a base substance at high temperature and spinning it into fibres with a binder added to provide rigidity. It is vapour and air permeable due to its structure. Moisture can build up in the insulant reducing its insulating value. May degrade over time. Lambda value 0.033–0.040 W/mK.

Glass wool
As for rock wool.

Health and safety
There is a health issue with fibrous materials. Some cause skin irritation and it is advisable to wear protective gear during installation. Loose fill fibre insulants should not be ventilated to internal habitable spaces. There has been the suggestion that fibrous materials constitute a cancer risk. However they are currently listed as 'not classifiable as to carcinogenicity in humans'.

Cellular

Cellular glass
Manufactured from natural materials and over 40 per cent recycled glass. It is impervious to water vapour and waterproof, dimensionally stable, noncombustible, vermin-proof and has high compressive strength as well as CFC and HCFC free. Lambda value 0.037–0.047 depending on particular application. Typical proprietary brand: Foamglas by Pittsburgh Corning (UK) Ltd.

Vermiculite
Vermiculite is the name given to a group of geological materials that resemble mica. When subject to high temperature the flakes of vermiculite expand due to their water content to many times their original size to become 'exfoliated vermiculite'. It has a high insulation value, resistant to decay, odourless, and non-irritant.

Organic/synthetic insulants are confined to cellular structure:
EPS (expanded polystyrene)
Rigid, flame retardant cellular, non-toxic, vapour resistant plastic insulation CFC and HCFC free.
Lambda value 0.032–0.040 W/mK

XPS (extruded polystyrene)
Closed cell insulant water and vapour tight, free from CFCs and HCFCs,
Lambda value 0.027–0.036 W/mK

PIR (polyisocyanurate)
Cellular plastic foam, vapour tight, available CFC and HCFC free
Lambda value 0.025–0.028

Phenolic
Rigid cellular foam very low Lambda value, vapour tight, good fire resistance, available CFC and HCFC free.
Lambda value 0.018–0.019 W/mK

In general, cellular materials do not pose a health risk and there are no special installation requirements.

Natural/organic insulants:
Fibre structure:
Cellulose
Mainly manufactured from recycled newspapers. Manufactured into fibres, batts or boards. Treated with fire retardant and pesticides.
Lambda value 0.038–0.040 W/mK

Sheep's wool
Must be treated with boron and a fire retardant. Disposal may have to be at specified sites.
Lambda value 0.040 W/mK

Flax
Treated with polyester and boron
Lambda value 0.037 W/mK

Straw
Heat-treated and compressed into fibre boards. Treated with fire retardant and pesticide. It can be used as a wall material with a high thermal efficiency. Hopefully in its present day form it will be much more reliable than the strawboard of the 1960s.
Lambda value 0.037 W/mK

Hemp
Under development as a compressed insulation board. A highly ecofriendly material, grows without needing pesticides and produces no toxins. Initial tests have used hemp as a building material mixed with lime and placed like concrete. Test houses have proved as

thermally efficient as identical well-insulated brick built houses built alongside the hemp examples.

Main points

Insulation materials should be free from HFCs and HCFCs,

- The choice of insulation material is governed primarily by two factors: thermal conductivity and location in the home. These points are considered further in Chapters 3 and 4.
- The ecological preference is for materials derived from organic or recycled sources and which do not use high levels of energy during production. However, there are certain overriding factors which will be described below.

The building fabric – roofs and lofts

Eco-renovation of a home is most cost effective when it is linked to necessary refurbishment, such as the renewal of tiles on a roof or external rendering. However, it is important to understand that thermal upgrading of a property might come under building control regulations. The Building Regulations for England and Wales, Part L 2002 include provisions which have a major impact on existing houses by setting insulation standards for any work which constitutes a major alteration. The term 'major alteration' includes:

- substantial replacement of any part of a roof including retiling and refelting
- significant changes to a floor including changing joists or re-boarding
- changes to an exposed wall, including renewing external render or internal plaster
- replacement doors, windows and rooflights
- replacement heating systems, including boilers and hot water systems
- heating and hot water controls
- instructions for heating systems must be provided and systems correctly commissioned.

The responsibility for compliance with the Building Regulations rests with the person ordering the work.

The thermal efficiency of a component of a building, such as a roof or wall, is described as its U-value. This is a measure of thermal transmittance, that is, the rate at which a composite element of a structure like a wall or window transmits heat. Technically it denotes the speed with which heat is lost through 1 m^2 of the element, when the difference in temperature between the inside and outside face of the element is 1°C. The lower the number, the higher its thermal efficiency. It is denoted by W/m^2K. It should not be confused with the conduction value (Lambda) which refers to a specific material like an insulant.

In a home without insulation about 25 per cent of its heat is lost through the roof. To repeat, this is the zone where the most cost-effective insulation investment can be made. The options are either a warm or a cold loft. The former is necessary if activities are to take place in the space or it is used for storage.

As mentioned, if there is a material alteration to the roof, insulation will need to be installed to a maximum U-value (W/m²K) according to the regulations:

pitched roof with insulation between the rafters (warm loft) or fixed to the face of rafters	0.20
pitched roof with insulation between or over ceiling joists (cold loft)	0.16
flat roof	0.25

Note: 'Maximum' in the context of U-values means the highest figure that is allowed which means the lowest level of permitted thermal efficiency. So, the higher the number, the poorer the thermal performance.

In cold lofts it is essential to ensure that the insulation is wrapped around water tanks with the space below the tank remaining uninsulated (Figure 3.1). All water pipes also must be insulated.

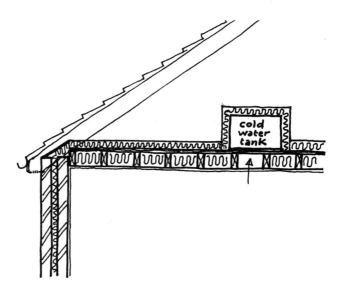

Figure 3.1
Cold loft and insulated water tank and all pipework.

In the case of inhabited lofts in most situations it is necessary to insert a vapour barrier between the insulation and the plasterboard internal finish. However, some insulants claim to render a vapour barrier unnecessary, for example Foamglas. Insulation board backed by aluminium foil is the most efficient (Figure 3.2).

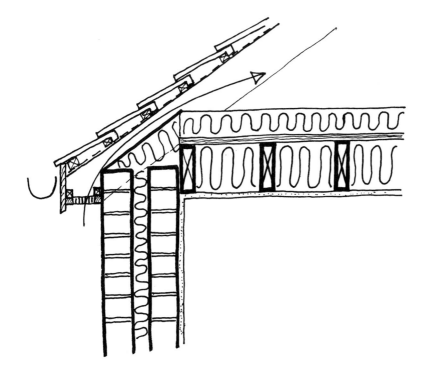

Figure 3.2
Insulation for a cold loft.

Insulants for lofts

Between and above floor joists

Fibre-based insulants are the most appropriate such as glass wool, rock wool, cellulose and sheep's wool. Thermafleece sheep's wool insulation from Second Nature has received an Agreement Certificate which confirms compliance with the Building Regulations require-ments for roof and timber-framed insulation. Excel Fibre Technology of Ebbw Vale produces Warmcel-RF from recycled newsprint. The fibre is pumped into the loft space by specialists. The fibre is produced by a low energy mechanical process which returns the newsprint into its original fibrous state (www.house-builder.co.uk).

If there is a risk of moisture infiltration in a loft it is advisable to use cellular glass or one of the organic synthetic insulants.

Warm lofts

Here the cellular insulants should be applied, either mineral (cellular glass, e.g. Foamglas Wallboard) or one of the organic/synthetics (EPS, XPS, phenolic) (Figure 3.3).

If a roof is being totally renewed it may be preferable to place the insulant over the rafters, (such as Foamglas Readyboard) and

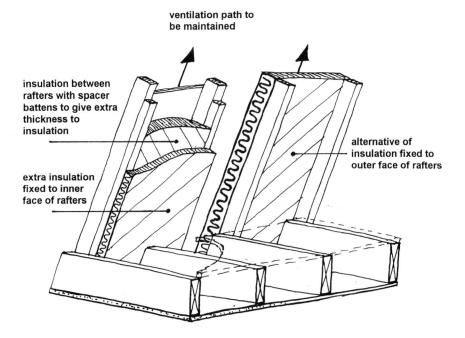

ventilation path to
be maintained

insulation between
rafters with spacer
battens to give extra
thickness to
insulation

alternative of
insulation fixed to
outer face of rafters

extra insulation
fixed to inner
face of rafters

Figure 3.3
Insulation for warm lofts.

fixed to the rafters and bonded together with a proprietary adhesive. Battens are fixed to the insulation board. A waterproof membrane is placed over the battens and finally counter-battens are fixed to support tiles/slates.

Note: It is important to ensure the ventilation gap of 50 mm between the eaves and the ridge is maintained to avoid condensation.

As a guide, to achieve a U-value of 0.2 W/m²K within the warm loft zone the thickness of insulation required is

Mineral wool, Lambda about 0.037	250 mm
Cellular insulants, Lambda about 0.022	220 mm

For a cold loft (U-value 0.16 W/m²K)

Mineral wool	275 mm
Cellular insulants	250 mm

Spray applied insulation

In some instances there are advantages to employing sprayed insulation. This is usually a two-part polyurethane foam which, when applied to the underside of a roof, bonds to slates or tiles and battens. It not only provides insulation, but also a waterproof barrier which firmly secures the slates/tiles in place. It expands on application to seal gaps preventing penetration by wind-driven rain or snow. The slates/tiles are also less prone to impact damage. The specialist contractor will advise on the requirements to meet the ventilation requirements under British Standard (BS) 5250 Control of Condensation in Buildings.

The insulation is applied to a thickness of 100 mm to satisfy the current Building Regulations to achieve the U-value of 0.16 W/m²K for cold lofts. One specialist installer which has received a BBA Certificate for Insulation (93/2939) is ISL Renotherm Ltd (Figure 3.4) (www.islrenotherm.co.uk).

Figure 3.4
Sprayed insulation by ISL Renotherm.

Flat roofs

Roofs with bituminous felt covering can be enhanced with rigid cellular insulation. It is possible to use felt-backed insulation panels which can then be finished with two further layers of felt or high performance single membrane.

Main points

- Insulating the loft heads the list of cost-effective insulation measures.

- It is first necessary to decide if the loft is to be a cold or warm space. If there it is to be an inhabited or storage space it must be warm.
- It would be prudent to opt for a warm loft to facilitate change of use in the future.
- In a cold loft the water storage tank should be insulated, except on the underside.
- The levels of insulation should conform to Part L of the Building Regulations.
- In most situations it is necessary to maintain at least a 50 mm ventilation path behind the insulation to avoid condensation.
- With specialized treatments, such as spray insulation, it is essential to use a qualified installer, preferably with a BBA Certificate for Insulation.

The building fabric – external walls and floors

Chapter Four

Cavity walls

In a typical inter-war suburban home around 35 to 45 per cent of its heat can be lost through its walls. Since about 1930, most houses in the UK have cavity wall construction. Approximately 75 per cent of houses in the UK still have not taken up the benefits of cavity insulation. It is claimed that the heat transfer through a cavity wall can be reduced by up to 63 per cent. Energy saving of between 19 and 35 per cent is possible if there is also loft insulation and the home is heated to the same standard as previously.

The process

Three materials meet the British Standard for cavity insulation. They are

- Rock wool
- Glass wool
- Expanded polystyrene beads.

Some installers include urea-formaldehyde foam which sets within the cavity into a meringue-like consistency. In the past there have been serious problems associated with off-gassing and providing pathways for damp around openings. It may be that these problems have been solved, but negative memories have a long shelf-life.

Insulation is blown into the cavity through holes about 20 mm diameter and 1.35 m apart.

Rock wool or glass wool are the most common insulants being stable over the lifetime of the building and impervious to moisture damage. In most cases cavities are about 50 mm wide, which means that a wall U-value W/m^2K can be achieved with:

- both leaves of brick   0.57
- outer leaf brick, inner leaf dense concrete block   0.54
- outer leaf brick, inner leaf lightweight concrete block   0.49

These values fall short of the 2002 Building Regulations standard for existing cavity wall houses of 0.45 W/m^{2}K. To reach this standard would require either internal dry lining insulation or external insulation as described below.

It is worth noting that the National Insulation Association claims that cavity insulation could, for most houses, achieve U-values between 0.38 and 0.43 W/m^{2}K. Before installing the insulation it is advisable that all wiring within the cavity is checked for compliance with current regulations by an accredited electrician. Underfloor ventilation should be safeguarded by sleeving air vents where necessary. After the operation all holes must be filled with matching mortar. The loose wool is blown into the cavity until it is tightly packed and will therefore not be subject to settlement. In semi-detached or terraced houses a brush barrier is placed in the cavity at the junction with an adjacent property.

It is impossible to give an accurate estimate of the payback time for this investment since it depends on location, the nature of the building fabric, the hours of heating and the comfort temperature set by the inhabitants. However, it is almost certainly within the range of 5–10 years.

As a rough guide, the cost of the operation at late 2002 prices should be:

3 bedroom detached house	£600
3 bedroom semi-detached house	£550
3 bed mid terrace house	£500
3 bedroom bungalow	£500

Quality control

In the past, there have been serious problems of quality control sometimes degenerating into criminal fraud. A number of steps should be taken to ensure a quality installation.

- Ensure that the insulation material being used and process employed are covered by a British Board of Agrément (BBA) certificate.
- Use installers whose work is regularly inspected and approved by the BBA.
- Confirm that the installation is guaranteed for 25 years under the Insulation Guarantee Agency, the government approved guarantee scheme. The guarantee covers defects in materials and workmanship which will be rectified without charge. The guarantee can be transferred to subsequent owners of the property.
- Choose an installer who is a member of the National Cavity Insulation Association (NCIA). The association should provide a list of approved installers.

As a precautionary footnote, in many older cavity wall homes it has been found that the wall ties connecting the two leaves have corroded in many cases to the point of disintegration. Before installing cavity insulation it would be wise to have a specialist check the state of the cavity so that, if necessary, new wall ties can be inserted.

Solid walls

In the UK, a large proportion of homes are either solid stone or 225 mm solid brickwork or concrete block. Solid walls were being built in some areas up to 1939. It is likely that a good number of home owners do not know whether they have a solid or cavity wall. This can be checked at window or door reveals. A plastered cavity wall should measure overall about 290 mm, whereas a solid brick wall will come to roughly 240 mm. If the exterior is rendered a further 18–25 mm should be added.

There are two ways of insulating solid external walls:

- by cladding the external face with insulation or 'overcladding'
- by fixing insulation to the internal face called 'dry lining'.

It is the first option which has the greater potential to achieve significant reductions in heat loss through the fabric. It also involves adjustments to several features of the fabric. However, one big advantage is that it can be applied without the house needing to be vacated.

Overcladding

Two methods of external insulation are available

- Fixing insulation board to the external face and finishing with a waterproof render
- A thick render coat containing an insulant sprayed or trowelled on to the wall surface.

The best results are obtained by the first option, insulation board fixed to the brickwork or blockwork. If a house is rendered it may be necessary to make good the surface to provide a sound fixing for the insulation board. If the backing wall substrate is sound and offers a clean, regular surface the insulation board can be fixed with adhesive. Otherwise mechanical fixing is necessary. For the operation to make a significant impact on heating bills, it will usually be necessary to have at least 100 mm of insulation. This will have implications for several external features which will need to be modified:

- If the roof eaves do not overhang sufficiently to accommodate the extra wall width, there will have to be modifications, for example by having an extended gutter which forms a closer to the insulation.
- To avoid cold bridges at openings, the insulation should also cover window and door reveals, which means that windows and doors may need to be replaced or modified. A cold bridge or thermal bridge is where there is discontinuity in the insulation resulting in a section of wall being colder than its surroundings. This attracts condensation and staining.
- Rainwater pipes and soil drain pipes will also have to be modified or boxed-in by the insulation. As a compromise it may be possible to insert thinner insulation boards behind fall pipes, but this does run the risk of cold bridging. The position of open and back inlet gullies may have to be modified. This can be very costly, and a compromise would be to insert a 'swan neck' section to the fall pipes at their base to bring them back to the face of the masonry wall. This will mean modifying the insulation at this point.
- Attention must be paid to the damp proof course (dpc) to ensure that the insulation backing does not cause dampness due to capillary action bypassing the dpc.

Quality control

The body that is recognized by government as the national trade association for the external cladding industry is the Insulated Render and Cladding Association (INCA). An installer (Figure 4.1) who is a member of the association is covered by an Agrément Certificate and the association offers a 10-year guarantee for the product and workmanship. At the same time installer members of INCA offer certified systems which have been granted a 25–30 year life. This ambiguity needs to be resolved (Insulated Render and Cladding Association Ltd, PO Box 12, Haslemere, Surrey GU27 3HA; www.inca-ltd.org.uk; Tel: 01428 654011.)

Some individual manufacturers offer a service which is covered by an Agrément Certificate, such as Pittsburgh Corning which describes itself as a 'Total Quality organization, working under ISO 9002' (the international standard). Its main product is 'FOAMGLAS' which is a cellular glass insulant. As indicated earlier, cellular glass is CFC- and HCFC-free, is impervious to any form of moisture, fireproof, dimensionally stable, gives off no toxic fumes, has high compressive strength and is proof against rot, vermin and insect infestation (www.foamglas.co.uk/building).

An alternative is StoTherm External Wall Insulation Systems which uses EPS insulation guaranteed CFC- HCFC-free. It offers insurance-backed cover for up to 10 years on adhesion, weather-proofing, cracking and colour fading (www.sto.co.uk).

As a guide to the thermal efficiency of various thicknesses of insulation applied externally to a 140 mm solid masonry wall plastered internally should be a U-value in W/m²K of:

Figure 4.1
Members of INCA fixing insulation and applying trowelled final coat of render.

65 mm insulation	0.45 (minimum in N.Ireland)
90 mm insulation	0.35 (Current Building Regulations England and Wales)
105 mm insulation	0.3 (pending Building Regulations in England and current in Scotland)
120 mm insulation	0.27 (Republic of Ireland)

External finish

It is necessary for the insulation boards to receive a finishing coat. In the case of most insulants the finish should offer total waterproofing. A polymer-based render is the most reliable in this respect. This is an adhesive render with an alkali-resistant glass fibre mesh as reinforcement. Applied in one or two coats offering a choice of finishes, for example:

Figure 4.2
External cladding being installed to solid wall homes, Penwith Housing Association.

- pebble dash or spar dash
- textured renders in a range of colours
- roughcast, also called harling or wet cast.

It is also possible to use cladding which include

- Lightweight natural stone aggregate
- Brick
- Tile, e.g. terracotta
- Weatherboarding

Traditional render systems around 25 mm thick consist of a base coat and top coat to comply with BS 5262. These systems normally require a metal lath carrier and can receive a mineral or synthetic finish.

Penwith Housing Association in Penzance, Cornwall took over the housing stock of the borough, much of which was solid masonry construction. It took the decision to overclad using the M.R. Swisslab system (Figures 4.2 and 4.3). This system offers a comprehensive service, including aluminium flashings to cover the insulation at eaves level and extension cills for windows.

The insulation is 70 mm of phenolic foam finished with a polymer cement render. Situated on the south west tip of the UK, these houses are exposed to extreme weather. The result of the upgrading has been a significant improvement in comfort levels and savings in space heating costs (www.alumasc-exteriors.co.uk; E-mail: info@alumasc-exteriors.co.uk; Helpline: 01744 648400).

Cost guidance

It is only possible to offer general guidance since each home is a special case. According to the Insulated Render and Cladding Association an overcladding project costs between £45 and £65/m² as at the end of 2002. For a semi-detached house with about 80 m² of wall area, this translates to between £3500 and £5500.

Benefits

- There is a significant improvement in comfort levels throughout the whole house.
- The walls of the building are protected from weathering, ensuring a longer life.
- There should be absolute protection from penetration by damp.
- The incidence of condensation is reduced to near zero.
- It allows the fabric of the home to act as a heat store – a warmth accumulator.
- It stabilizes the structure, preventing cracking due to differential thermal expansion.

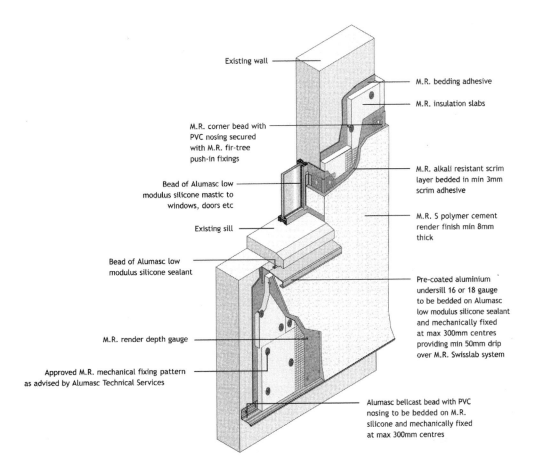

Existing wall

M.R. bedding adhesive

M.R. insulation slabs

M.R. corner bead with PVC nosing secured with M.R. fir-tree push-in fixings

Bead of Alumasc low modulus silicone mastic to windows, doors etc

Existing sill

Bead of Alumasc low modulus silicone sealant

M.R. render depth gauge

Approved M.R. mechanical fixing pattern as advised by Alumasc Technical Services

M.R. alkali resistant scrim layer bedded in min 3mm scrim adhesive

M.R. S polymer cement render finish min 8mm thick

Pre-coated aluminium undersill 16 or 18 gauge to be bedded on Alumasc low modulus silicone sealant and mechanically fixed at max 300mm centres providing min 50mm drip over M.R. Swisslab system

Alumasc bellcast bead with PVC nosing to be bedded on M.R. silicone and mechanically fixed at max 300mm centres

- Space heating bills can be reduced by up to 50 per cent.
- The increase in property value as a result of the upgrading usually more than offsets the cost.
- There is normally a significant improvement in appearance.
- The operation can be undertaken without the need to vacate the property.
- There is a significant reduction in carbon dioxide emissions. Government estimates suggest that, over the lifetime of the building, one tonne of CO_2 is saved for every square metre of 50 mm thick insulation

Figure 4.3
M.R. Swisslab system application details. Courtesy of Alumasc Exterior Buildings Products Ltd.

A company which claims to be the world's leading manufacturer of the combination of external insulation and finishes is Dryvit Systems Inc. Dryvit UK Ltd is a wholly owned subsidiary. Its standard system is called 'Outsulation' (Figure 4.4). Its 'Roxsulation' system incorporates mineral wool insulation. It is BBA approved. Care needs to be taken that it conforms to the latest version of Part L of the Building Regulations. As a guide the mineral wool insulation board

Figure 4.4
Dryvit external cladding system installed at Baggy House, UK.

system has a thermal conductivity of 0.036 WmK which compares favourably with expanded polystyrene (www.dryvit.co.uk; E-mail: ukenquiries@dryvit.com; Tel: 01462 819555).

Sprayed insulation

Sprayed application of a two-part polyurethane foam is another possibility. ISL Renotherm claims that 45 mm of foam can bring an external wall up a U-value of 35 W/m²K which is the current Building Regulation standard. It is about to receive a BBA Certificate for this application (www.islrenotherm.co.uk).

Internal insulation (dry lining)

Where it is not practical to adopt cavity or external insulation, the only option is to revert to dry lining. The dilemma is that it reduces internal space. To bring a 140 mm solid external wall up the Buildings Regulations standard would require at least 90 mm of insulation with a plasterboard finish. A suitable insulant is cellular glass fixed to the wall

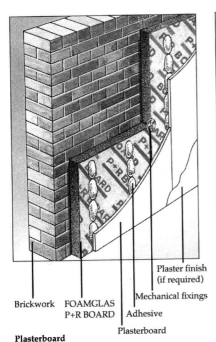

Brickwork FOAMGLAS
P+R BOARD

Plaster finish
(if required)

Mechanical fixings

Adhesive

Plasterboard

Plasterboard

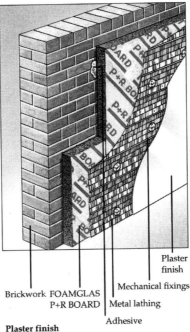

Brickwork FOAMGLAS
P+R BOARD

Plaster
finish

Mechanical fixings

Metal lathing

Adhesive

Plaster finish

Figure 4.5
Dry lining using Foamglas P+R
board with plasterboard or
plaster finish. Courtesy of
Pittsburgh Corning (UK) Ltd.

mechanically. The finish is either plasterboard with a skim coat of plaster or plaster applied to metal lathing. There are consequences to using this system, such as the relocation of skirtings and electrical sockets. There is also the risk of cold bridging if the insulation is not continued around the reveals to openings. This could involve the replacement of external doors and windows. However this is one instance where the best can be the enemy of the good and compromise is reasonable. The recommended U-value for dry-lined external walls is 0.45 W/m²K (Figure 4.5).

Party walls could benefit from dry lining treatment, not necessarily to the thickness of external walls. Not only will this conserve warmth, it would also reduce noise transmission.

A typical 19th century terraced house could benefit from a combination of overcladding and dry lining. The front of the house, which is often at the back or the pavement, would not be suitable for overcladding, making dry lining the only option. However, the rear, which is often L-shaped in plan, could receive overcladding treatment. This is best undertaken on a whole street basis if possible to avoid discontinuity and to realize the benefits of economy of scale.

Floors

Suspended floors with underfloor ventilation are a prime source of heat loss. For ground floors and basements the recommended U-

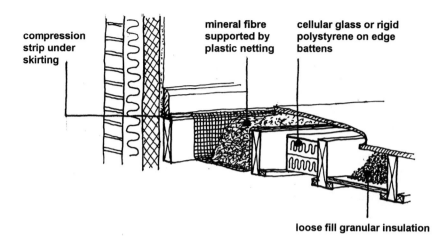

compression strip under skirting

mineral fibre supported by plastic netting

cellular glass or rigid polystyrene on edge battens

loose fill granular insulation

Figure 4.6
Floor insulation options.

value is 0.25 W/m²K. The most common method is to insert the insulation between the floor joists. If there is insufficient crawl space below the joists there is no alternative but to remove the floor boards or sheet covering to achieve a meaningful degree of insulation. The easiest method is to lay plastic netting over the joists and then fill to floor board level with a mineral fibre insulant. Alternatively, battens and a tray can be fixed to the joists allowing a loose fill insulant to be used. Another option is to simply fix battens to the bottom of the joists and use a rigid polystyrene or cellular glass insulant.

Skirting boards should be checked for draughts. If there is an underfloor void it is surprising how much cold air can penetrate the habitable space due to an inadequate seal between skirtings and floorboards (Figure 4.6).

For solid concrete floors there is no alternative but to place the insulation material on top of the slab. To realize a meaningful improvement in thermal efficiency will necessitate raising the floor level by at least 80 mm using a rigid insulant, such as cellular glass. Ideally the floor covering should be removed exposing the screed. It may be necessary to make good the screed with a sand and cement mix to achieve a smooth, level surface. An insulant with high compressive strength such as 'Foamglas floorboard' is then laid on the screed. A polyethylene vapour barrier must be laid over the insulation and beneath a chipboard subfloor. The finish is optional.

Where it is not feasible to raise the floor level by 80 mm or so, a compromise expedient is to lay 5 mm cork tiles. Cork has good insulation properties.

Windows and doors

Many home owners elect to replace windows as much for cosmetic as thermal reasons. It is an expensive operation and, in terms of

(b)

Figure 4.7
Swedish windows installed (a) in improvement works to flat in Chelmsford, UK; and (b) during the eco-refurbishment of a house in Cumbria, UK.

(a)

saved energy, the payback time could be up to 15 years. However, this may be more than offset by the increase in the value of the property. This will especially be the case when houses will require an energy rating at the point of sale.

Under the 2002 Building Regulations replacement windows must conform to Part L of the Building Regulations unless there are compelling reasons for a waiver, for example in the case of listed buildings. These state that windows, doors and rooflights in a timber or PVCu frame must have a maximum U-value of 2.00 W/m²K. It is also advisable to have a minimum of a 12 mm gap between the panes of the double glazing. On this basis double glazing with argon-gas filling and soft low-E coating meets the standard.

If metal frames are necessary perhaps because of the character of the house, or its listed status, the maximum U-value is 2.2 W/m²K. In this case triple glazing with air filling and hard low-E coating is the required specification, plus the fact that thermal breaks must be included in the frames to reduce heat loss through the metal. For the ultimate in triple glazing there is the Swedish Window Company, www.swedishwindows.com (Figure 4.7).

A high quality double-glazed window is marketed by Construction Resources. Frames are constructed from the heartwood of slow-growing Scandinavian fir trees that are 120–150 years old. The glass is argon-filled double glazing with Low-E glass producing a U-value of 1.4 W/m²K. The windows are finished in water-based paints to a variety of colours. They can be delivered untreated. (www.constructionresources.com; Email: sales@ecoconstruct.com).

Timber is the preferred choice for window frames. Whilst softwoods gained a poor reputation in the 1960s and 1970s they are now mostly more reliable. Hardwoods should be from an authenticated sustainable source, preferably native to the UK. PVC frames are ecologically damaging, especially since the manufacturing process involves the use of chlorine.

Helplines

Grants are available for installing insulation and draught proofing from the UK Government's Warm Front scheme. Grants up to £1500 are available to households with children under 16 and pregnant women who are on income-related or disability benefit. Grants of up to £2500 are available to anyone aged over 60 who is on income-related benefit. In the Yorkshire and Humberside, Eastern and East Midlands areas the Warm Front scheme is administered by TXU Warm Front (www.txuwarmfront.co.uk; Tel: 0800 952 1555). The remainder of the UK scheme is administered by the Energy Action Grants Agency (EAGA) (www.eaga.co.uk; Tel: 0800 316 6011).

Pensioners are entitled to a winter fuel payment of £200. Information on www.thepensionservice.gov.uk/winterfuel; Tel: 08459 151515.

The charity Age Concern offers a 'Help with Heating' fact sheet (www.ageconcern.org.uk; Tel: 0800 00 99 66).

Help the Aged provides a fact sheet 'Keep out the Cold' (www.helptheaged.org.uk; Tel: 0808 800 6565).

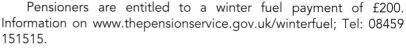

Main points

- Check if external walls are cavity construction and if so whether they already have received insulation.
- If not, install cavity fill insulation such as rock wool, glass wool or polystyrene beads, first checking cavity for corroded wall ties or blockages.
- Use an accredited installer such as a member of the National Cavity Insulation Association.
- Check guarantee.
- In the case of solid masonry walls, the options are overcladding or dry lining, or a combination of both.
- For overcladding it is advisable to use a contractor who is a member of the Insulated Render and Cladding Association.
- The maximum possible thickness of insulation should be applied,

preferably 120 mm if circumstances allow. The marginal cost of going for the best is soon repaid in lower heating bills.

- External finishes should be watertight and conform to British Standard 5262. There is a wide choice of finishes.
- If the property is listed or in a conservation area it will be necessary to consult the local Planning Department, since there is likely to be a significant change in appearance.
- Internal dry lining should give a solid wall a U-value of at least 0.45 W/m^{2}K.
- Well-insulated floors give good value in terms of insulation and comfort. If floor boards are being replaced the opportunity should not be missed to fill the joist spaces with insulation. If there is adequate space under the joists, then insulation can easily be installed from below.
- For solid floors the least disruptive option is to lay 5-mm cork tiles.
- New external doors and windows should conform to current Building Regulations in terms of thermal efficiency. The ecological choice for windows is timber framing from a sustainable source.
- Explore the possibility of grants.

Chapter Five Draught proofing and ventilation

These two aspects of an upgrading strategy are intimately connected and therefore must be considered in conjunction with each other. Efficient draught proofing can be the most cost-effective first step towards energy efficiency since some older homes can lose up to 40 per cent of their warmth through air leakage. The worst villain of the piece is an open fire. Whilst it is a source of heat it is also a super-highway for removing warmth. An efficient draught-proofing campaign can cut space heating losses in an existing home by 25–35 per cent.

Infiltration of cold air occurs when the outside pressure is greater than internal pressure and there are pathways allowing the pressure to be equalized. The result is draughts. The main causes of pressure difference are:

- The effect of wind, exerting pressure on the windward side and suction on the leeward side. It can force cold air into a house, but also extract warmth from it (see Figure 5.5, p. 37).
- The consequences of combustion. Open fires and gas cookers usually draw their oxygen for combustion from the living space, creating a negative pressure.
- Extract fans in kitchens and bathrooms lower internal pressure.
- Warm air is lighter than cold air and therefore rises relative to the cold air – the 'stack effect'. The easiest escape route is the open fire flue. Also leakage through a hatch to a cold roof space is a culprit, especially if the loft is uninsulated. This creates higher pressure at the top of the house forcing warm air to be expelled, whilst lower pressure at ground level draws cold air into the property. The stack effect naturally increases with the number of storeys. Most houses have vertical pathways which allow warm air to rise. This is especially the case in timber-framed properties. Stud partitions may also provide subtle routes for rising air, as do butt-jointed floorboards. Skirting boards should be checked for draughts. Staircases are an obvious major pathway, especially in open plan homes where the stairs commence from the living space; so too are vertical ducts carrying pipework.

Before embarking on a draught-proofing strategy it is important to understand that a near airtight house needs assisted ventilation. The guide is that a ventilation system should provide at least a third air changes per hour (ACH). It must also be remembered that flame appliances need combustion air. This is especially important in the case of gas appliances. The regulations state that where there is a gas appliance which draws its combustion air from habitable spaces there must be a permanent ventilation vent to the exterior, which, of course, conflicts with draught proofing. This dilemma will be considered in the section on heating appliances.

From diagnosis to remedy

Windows and doors

In the case of windows it is not just opening lights which can admit draughts. Frequently the seals round fixed lights are deficient and it is worth making a physical check round the frames when there is an adequate wind blowing – say force 4 on the Beaufort Scale – which causes significant movement in trees. Resealing with a silicon compound is the answer.

However, it is opening lights which are the main problem, and some are more permeable than others, as, for example, the traditional sash window. The weakest point is where the upper and lower panes meet. Here brush type draught stripping attached to the meeting rails is the best option. Brush strips are also necessary within the head and side frames.

In the 1960s and 1970s, centre pivot windows were popular. Besides the normal perimeter stripping they need special attention at the hinge since the nature of the design creates a significant gap. Compression type draught strips are the preferred option here, fixed to the rebate of the window frame and to the angled rebates in the opening lights.

In that era metal sliding windows were also in vogue. Wherever there is lateral movement, brush type strip is appropriate. All sides need the brush treatment with special attention given to the vertical meeting stiles.

The most common type of opening light is the side hung casement window. All the frame rebates need compression strips. The same goes for top hung opening windows.

Doors

Most external doors are inward opening, making them a particular draught problem. Because of wear and tear the heavy duty brush type is advisable in this context. However, the most efficient strategy

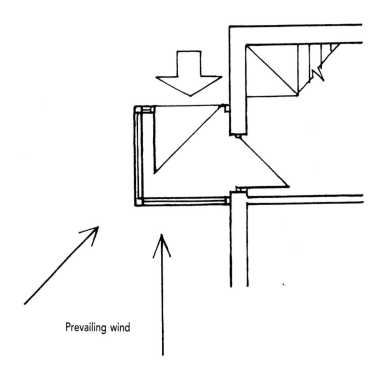

Figure 5.1
Porch/draught lobby.

Prevailing wind

is more radical. It is well worth considering a draught lobby/porch addition to the main entrance. It has numerous amenity values besides being an efficient form of insulation. The important point to consider is that the porch door should be at right angles to the main door, if possible opposite to the prevailing wind (Figure 5.1).

Sliding patio doors benefit from brush strips to all frame rebates and at the meeting stiles. Doors to unheated basements should be treated as external doors.

Open fires

The traditional open fire has considerable appeal, not least for its primordial symbolism. It is also the most inefficient heat source sending most of its warmth up the chimney. At the same time it consumes huge quantities of air which must by replaced either directly or through infiltration. When the fire is not functioning, the chimney, as mentioned, provides a ready escape route for rising warm air. Various remedies are described in Chapter 6.

Ventilation

As stated above, the average home needs at least a third to a half ACH to maintain reasonable freshness. An effective draught-proofing strategy will cut off the traditional ventilation routes. This can be hazardous where there are flame appliances that rely for combustion oxygen on air from the habitable space. (To repeat: the regulations require all such appliances to have direct access to external air.) If a gas or oil burning appliance has insufficient oxygen for efficient burning, toxic gases can accumulate to a level at which they can prove fatal. Special ventilation measures are necessary when the natural ventilation rate is less than 0.35 ACH.

How do you find out if your home is above or below the line in terms of infitration ventilation? The answer is pressure testing. An external door is removed and a panel inserted which allows air to be forced into the building until the pressure reaches 50 Pa. Then the rate at which that pressure needs to be sustained gives an accurate account of the extent of leakage. However, this is an elaborate process which, for an existing home, might seem excessive. The safe bet is to assume that if rigorous draught sealing has been undertaken then special ventilation measures are necessary.

These can take the form either of stack ventilation or mechanically assisted ventilation. As a general rule, a fan assisted system would move about 1.6 m^3 per min (15 ft^3). So, for a fairly large home of 232 m^2 (2500 ft^2) and 2.44 m (8 ft) ceilings, the system would need to move about 20 m^3 per minute.

In the case of natural stack ventilation it is usually the case that the design of a building has to be adapted to this technology from the outset. In a retrofit situation it is usually necessary to employ mechanically assisted ventilation with heat recovery. The technical terms are either energy recovery ventilators (ERVs) or heat recovery ventilators (HRVs). For an average semi-detached house, the electricity consumed by the fans is about the same as a 100 W light bulb. This has to be offset against the heating energy being saved, usually about 1 to 2 kW per hour. On average the HRV recovers 60–75 per cent of the heat contained in the exhaust air, returning it to the interior.

HRV systems can have variable controls, allowing, for example, a high speed boost for bathrooms or utility rooms. They can control moisture levels and accommodate gas detectors. It is common practice to locate these systems in the loft space, with flexible tubular supply and return ducts to the living spaces. It is possible to have a small heating element in the supply duct to boost the recovered heat in really cold weather. The incoming supply ducts should be located as far as possible from sources of pollution, especially flues. Within the rooms linked to the system, supply and return vents should be at least 3 m apart (10 ft) (Figure 5.2).

This may all seem to be a rather complex and costly operation. In fact the benefits are considerable, aside from the obvious cost savings in space heating. For example, it will stabilize the pressure throughout the house, eliminating draughts. Often draughts are generated by a difference in temperature called a thermal gradient.

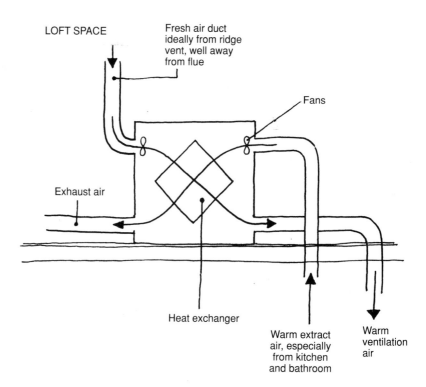

LOFT SPACE

Fresh air duct
ideally from ridge
vent, well away
from flue

Fans

Exhaust air

Heat exchanger

Warm extract
air, especially
from kitchen
and bathroom

Warm
ventilation
air

Figure 5.2
Cross-flow heat recovery
ventilation unit.

This can be readily experienced in cold weather by sensing the drop in temperature adjacent to windows. What is not so evident is that there can often be a significant difference in temperature between the lower and upper levels of a room, producing discomfort. HRV systems in a well-insulated home will ensure that there is only a 1 to 2°C difference between floor and ceiling.

For domestic purposes, a common type of HRV is the cross flow heat exchanger. The outgoing air transfers its heat to the incoming air across a series of metal plates (Figure 5.3).

Another mechanism is the thermal wheel HRV. Here a wheel containing a medium that can quickly absorb heat rotates. It collects heat from the outgoing stream and transfers it to the incoming air. It is one of the most efficient of all the HVR systems (Figure 5.4).

Air leakage through ventilated roofs

According to Professor Farshad Alamdari of the UK Building Research Establishment (BRE) 'on average approximately 30 per cent of total space heating losses in a house occur through the roof section'. This statement was made in the context of a BRE research study into a comparison between traditional ventilated roofs and nonventilated

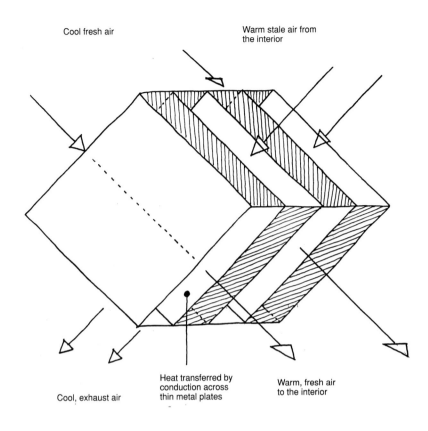

Cool fresh air

Warm stale air from
the interior

Cool, exhaust air

Heat transferred by
conduction across
thin metal plates

Warm, fresh air
to the interior

Figure 5.3
Detail of cross-flow heat
exchanger.

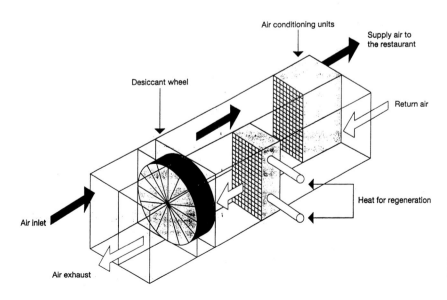

Air conditioning units

Supply air to
the restaurant

Desiccant wheel

Return air

Heat for regeneration

Air inlet

Air exhaust

Figure 5.4
Thermal wheel heat transfer.

proprietary systems. The main reason for ventilating the roof space is to remove condensation. The system used in the study was the Du Pont Tyvek® sealed roof boards. It found that these vapour permeable boards reduced condensation in winter to a mere 12 g/m^2 per day which is easily dispersed through diffusion through the breathable Tyvek membrane. Compared with a conventional roof, air leakage in the test house was reduced by 74 per cent. Expressed as air changes per hour (ach), these were down to 1.7 ach compared with the conventional control house of 6 ach.

Reducing ventilation losses also has energy implications. According to John Hart of BRE the sealed roof system reduced the space heating demand in the test house by 927 kWh over the heating season. It is also claimed that, over the lifetime of the boards, a typical house will save 6 tonnes of CO_2, as well as being fully recyclable.

Tyvek is distributed in the UK by Owens Corning Alcopor (www.owenscorning.com or www.alcopor.com; OCA Advisory Service: Freefone 0800 627425).

The external environment

Concerns:

- Wind
- Rain
- Solar shading
- Evaporative cooling.

The UK has one of the most turbulent climates in Europe. In the UK the average wind speed for 10 per cent of the time ranges from 8 to about 12.5 m per second, the higher figures being in Scotland. At the same time, average wind speeds increase by 7 per cent for every 100 m increase in altitude.

The orientation, as well as the location of a property, can have a significant impact on the extent to which it is adversely affected by wind. As previously mentioned, wind creates a pressure difference on the faces of a building, positive on the windward side and negative on the leeward face (Figure 5.5). This means that cold air tends to be forced into the windward elevation and warmth sucked out of the lee side. The infiltration is naturally going to increase with wind speed. This will have an impact on temperature since winter westerly winds tend to be warm, whilst northerlies and easterlies are cold.

Wind speeds can be considerably reduced by the introduction of natural or artificial dampeners. A solid wind break can greatly reduce wind speed in its immediate vicinity but beyond that zone will cause turbulence. On the other hand, an openwork fence with only

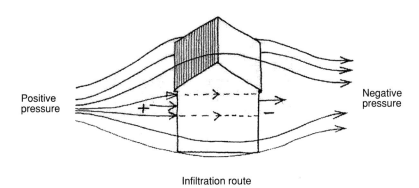

Positive
pressure

Negative
pressure

Infiltration route

Figure 5.5
Wind pressure and infiltration.

50 per cent solid resistance to wind will moderate wind speed over a much greater area. At the same time, a timber fence of this nature will be less likely to become a casualty of gale force winds.

Natural features can be effective wind breaks. Even low level planting creates drag, thereby slowing the wind force. Trees are the best option, remembering that deciduous trees are much less effective in winter. As a rule of thumb, the distance from a house to a tree break should be four to five times the height of the trees to optimize the dampening effect.

Climatologists predict that global warming will result in wetter winters and much drier summers with droughts a regular occurrence. This gives shrubs and trees a further benefit in the degree to which they protect from the drying or desiccating effect of wind. According to the TV gardening personality Monty Don, 'In the British climate, wind is far more of a problem than sunshine and can be drought-inducing in the middle of winter when there is not a ray of sunshine to be seen for days' (*Observer Magazine*, 19 January 2003).

Wind plus driving rain can affect the thermal efficiency of a property. When brickwork becomes saturated the thermal conductivity of brickwork or blockwork increases since moist masonry transmits heat more effectively than in a dry condition. This problem would be cured with a polymer-based render.

Main points

- Older homes can lose up to 40 per cent of their heat through leakage.
- Open fires are a rapid exit route for warmth when not in use.
- Target even the most unlikely places, like skirting boards, for draught sealing treatment.
- For open flame gas appliances it is mandatory to supply combustion air from the outside.

- A comprehensive draught sealing strategy will necessitate low energy mechanical ventilation with heat recovery.
- A porch can be beneficial if its door is at right angles to the house door and opposite the prevailing wind.
- Infiltration of draughts is reinforced by wind. The external environment can reduce the impact of winds through tree and shrub planting and openwork timber fences. Even low shrubs have a dampening effect on wind speed.

Heating

Chapter Six

This chapter is concerned primarily with space heating. Any funda-
mental modifications to a home heating regime should wait until after
the programme of draught sealing and insulation has been
completed. This is because the heating load should have been
considerably reduced.

Taking first the conventional open fire, this, as has been stated,
is an effective means of removing heat from rooms. Not only does it
draw in air for combustion, it is also a thermal chimney, pulling air
from the home through the stack effect. Some fireplaces have a flap
which can close the flue when the fire is not in use.

In Germany, the answer has been to provide ducted air from the
outside to the fireplace. The front of the fire is sealed by a glass door.
In the UK some proprietary open fires incorporate ducted air. The most
efficient alternative is a closed stove with glass doors which provides
both radiant and convection heat with ducted access to outside air. An
advantage is that such stoves can burn a variety of fuels.

For a gas fire, the most thermally efficient is that which is glass
fronted and has a balanced flue. This is a single horizontal duct to
the exterior which provides combustion air, whilst also expelling
exhaust gases. Some open gas fires offer the facility of a duct to the
external wall. This type draws combustion air from the living space
whilst exhaust air is mechanically expelled through the horizontal
duct. The problem with this type is that, when the fire is not lit, the
duct provides a clear passage for the ingress of cold air and when it
is lit it forcibly extracts the hot flue gases without the option of
providing convection heat. The final downside is that it requires a
permanent vent to the outside for combustion air.

Central heating

In the domestic sector, most systems consist of either the wet or
ducted warm air variety. Some examples of electric underfloor
heating still persist in the UK despite being the least economical and

environmentally responsible of all systems. As regards the wet systems there are three aspects which can benefit from upgrading treatment. The first is the boiler. If a boiler is at or near the point of being replaced, it is advisable to install a condensing boiler. This exploits the flue gases to give an efficiency improvement of about 20 per cent over a conventional boiler. How this works is that combustion gases contain steam from the burning of natural gas which is cooled by the return water from the central heating. This condenses releasing its latent heat. In the UK it is important that the appliance is installed by a CORGI registered operative. On a cautionary note, it has been claimed that 'after a very short time in operation cheap condensing boilers do not condense' (Liddell and Grant, 2002: 12). Since such changes should take place after the property has been insulated and draught proofed, it is important that the boiler should be sized according to the revised rate of heat loss.

The second aspect concerns the radiators. Modern systems use small bore flow and return pipes of 15 or 22 mm diameter. Hot water is pumped under pressure to each radiator through flow and return pipes connected to a common manifold. Not only does this maximize efficiency, it also enables radiators to be isolated for maintenance. Older systems are of the single pipe variety and work by convection or gravity. The water in the system passes through each radiator in turn before returning to the boiler. If a system is due for replacement it is advisable to select a small bore or even a micro-bore system (12 or 6 mm diameter) with radiators which offer the maximum heated surface area. Where pipes are under the floor it is important for them to be insulated.

In older systems, high priority should be given to replacing simple on–off valves controlling radiators with the thermostatic variety. This enables the temperature of an individual radiator to be set at a level appropriate for its location. Foil-backed insulation board placed behind a radiator will significantly improve its efficiency.

It has long been the practice to place radiators below windows, since this is the situation which is most obviously cool. It is also the place which ensures that a radiator gives off much of its heat to the outer atmosphere. Far better to place radiators against inner walls. Where radiators do exist below windows it is essential to ensure that curtains fall behind the radiator.

The third factor concerns the room thermostat. It should be positioned in the main living area and away from direct sunlight. The conventional wisdom dictates that the system should be switched off overnight. Unless the construction of the house offers high thermal mass, this is not an ideal situation. It is important that the temperature in bedrooms should be maintained at a comfort level of about 18°C, especially for the elderly and infirm. This could be achieved by manually changing the thermostat setting each evening and morning. However, the smart solution is to fit a thermostat in the main bedroom coupled to a time clock which automatically switches from the living room thermostat to the night thermostat and then back to the day thermostat at appropriate times for the particular householder. This ensures that it is the bedrooms which have the optimum temperature.

Developments in technology now make available controls which can perform a variety of functions and which are able to learn to operate the system to maximum efficiency according to the habits of the occupants. It is also desirable to have a control system in which the central heating system operates in harmony with the heat recovery ventilation system. It is important to check that an installer is aware of the latest developments in boiler and control technology.

There is also a boiler thermostat which controls the running temperature of the unit. It is usually best to select a high setting for the sake of efficiency. It would be well to consult the manufacturer's user manual or seek specialist advice as to the optimum setting for the boiler in question.

When installing a new central heating system, the following may be a useful checklist.

- Ensure that the system is not over-designed, but matched to the size and thermal efficiency of the property.
- Select a boiler with electronic ignition; the traditional pilot light is wasteful.
- Ensure that the radiators and controls are 'state of the art' in terms of thermal efficiency and CO_2 rating.
- Spend time to become conversant with the instruction manuals in order to refine the system to best suit specific needs.
- Maintain the system regularly. Both the boiler and radiators need regular maintenance, the latter to ensure that air is bled from the system periodically.
- In the UK, use a CORGI registered installer.

The conservatory

This is a feature which is becoming increasingly popular, more for its amenity value than saving energy. If it is an addition, say, to a living room and therefore part of the living space it must conform to building regulations unless it can be fully closed off. The warmth generated in a conservatory can be used to supply warm air to the cold side of the house. The warm air must obviously be ducted from the highest point of the glazing. Alternatively water heated in a pipe painted matt black at the apex could supplement the domestic hot water supply. If there is no fan extract of warm air, then buoyancy circulation will occur with hot air rising and cooler air moving in to take its place. An advantage of a conservatory is that it contributes to the thermal mass of the building which can be particularly helpful if there is sunshine during winter months.

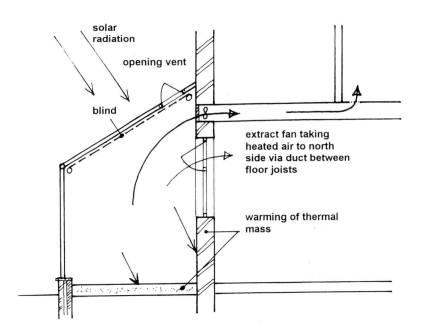

Figure 6.1
Conservatory with ducted solar heated air.

However, there are two notes of caution. First, there may be excessive solar gain so it is important to ensure that adequate solar blinds are fitted. Portable air conditioning units to provide cooling should be avoided at all costs. Second, in many cases the energy-saving benefits of a conservatory can be more than offset by the installation of heating to enable it to be a space for all seasons (Figure 6.1).

Main points

- When replacing a central heating boiler choose a high quality condensing boiler.
- Installation should be by a CORGI registered fitter.
- All radiators should be fitted with thermostatic valves.
- Reflective foil behind a radiator with its reflective face against the radiator improves performance.
- Ensure curtains fall behind a radiator.
- Consider replacing controls/thermostats to ensure that temperatures are appropriate for particular rooms at specific times, especially bedrooms.
- Conservatories should be regarded as sun spaces and not extensions of a living room to be heated in winter.
- Heat from a conservatory can be ducted to the cold side of a house, reducing the load on central heating.

Alternatives to conventional heating

Chapter Seven

In recent years, there have been significant advances in the technology for providing central heating in the domestic sector, with the additional benefit of generating electricity at the same time. These are sometimes referred to as home power units (HPUs) and they deliver combined heat and power or CHP. An alternative term is micro-cogeneration. One of the promising systems for homes is based on the Stirling engine.

Micro-CHP

It is interesting how two 19th century technologies, the fuel cell and the Stirling engine, are only now coming into their own. Invented by Robert Stirling in 1816, the engine that bears his name is described as an 'external combustion engine'. This is because heat is applied to the outside of the unit to heat up a gas within a sealed cylinder. The heat source is at one end of the cylinder, while the cooling takes place at the opposite end. The internal piston is driven by the successive heating and cooling of the gas. When the gas is heated it expands, pushing down the piston. In the process the gas is cooled and then pushed to the heated top of the cylinder by the returning piston, once again to expand and repeat the process. Because of advances in piston technology and in materials like ceramics from the space industry and high temperature steels allowing temperatures to rise to 1200°C, it is now considered a firm contender for the micropower market (Figure 7.1).

The operational principle is that a fixed amount of gas is sealed within the engine. In present day engines this is helium or nitrogen. It works on the basis that when the temperature of a specific amount of gas within a fixed volume of space is raised the pressure will increase. At the same time, compressing the gas within the fixed volume will raise its temperature. Heat is applied to the exterior of the engine to achieve this change of state of the gas. Heat can be drawn off the engine at its cool end to provide space heating for a

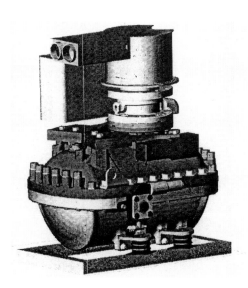

Figure 7.1
Dual chamber Stirling engine.

warm air or wet system. Alternatively it can supply domestic hot water. In some cases, the vertical motion of the piston is converted to circular motion to power a generator.

In the 2 March 2002 issue of the journal *New Scientist* it reported on a family in the UK operating a WhisperTech Stirling engine currently available from Gastec and Zantingh in The Netherlands. The family were satisfied that the unit served heating and hot water needs

Figure 7.2
Illustration of the WhisperGen arrangement in a typical house.

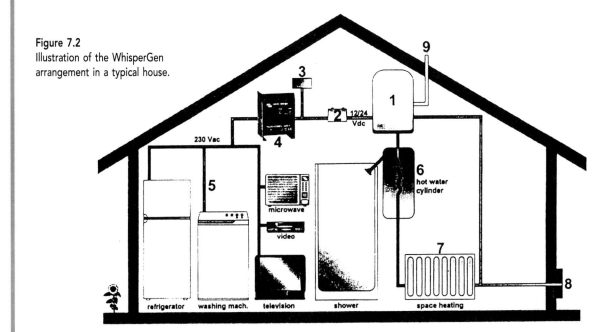

as effectively as a conventional boiler from a unit no larger than a domestic refrigerator. The bonus was the electricity. The system generates DC current which needs to be converted to AC via an inverter. This means that it can serve normal appliances and also export surplus electricity to the grid. At the same time, electricity can be imported from the grid at times of peak demand or when there is minimum demand for heat. The WhisperTech unit produces 6 kW of heat and 1 kW of electricity.

Another manufacturer is Victron Energy in The Netherlands. Its Stirling-based system goes under the name of WhisperGen (Figure 7.2). Electricity production is rated at 800 W (800 We) and available heat at 7 kW (7 kWh). It is designed to run on automotive diesel fuel (www.victronenergy.com).

The UK company BG Group is currently conducting trials of a Stirling CHP system under the name MicroGen. At the heart of the system is a unique technology developed by Sunpower in the USA. This consists of a sealed chamber containing a free piston integrated with an alternator. The piston carries the alternator magnets, enabling the production of single phase electricity at 230 volts (50 Hz).

The top of the chamber is heated to 550°C whilst the lower part is cooled to the heating system temperature (usually approximately 45°C) creating the necessary pressure difference in the captive gas. The MicroGen unit is designed to produce 1.1 kW of electricity, which is considered to be adequate for base load domestic requirements. Any further load will be drawn from the grid in the normal way. Because the system is strictly controlled to 50 Hz, it is compatible with mains electricity and therefore can be linked directly to the domestic ring main. It will be possible to feed excess electricity back to the grid. The four phases of the Stirling cycle are explained in Figure 7.3.

On the heating side, the heat which is drawn off by the water coolant is reinforced by heat from the flue gases extracted by a heat exchanger. There is a supplementary heating element in the system

Figure 7.3
Four phases of the Stirling engine cycle.

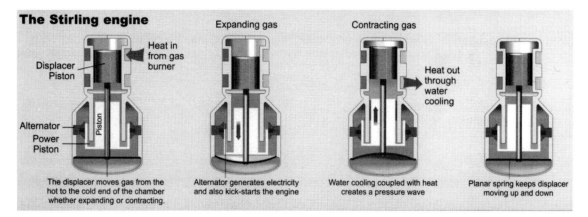

The Stirling engine

Displacer Piston

Heat in from gas burner

Alternator

Power Piston

Piston

The displacer moves gas from the hot to the cold end of the chamber whether expanding or contracting.

Expanding gas

Alternator generates electricity and also kick-starts the engine

Contracting gas

Heat out through water cooling

Water cooling coupled with heat creates a pressure wave

Planar spring keeps displacer moving up and down

Figure 7.4
(a) MicroGen Stirling CHP
system and (b) prototype of
wall mounted unit.

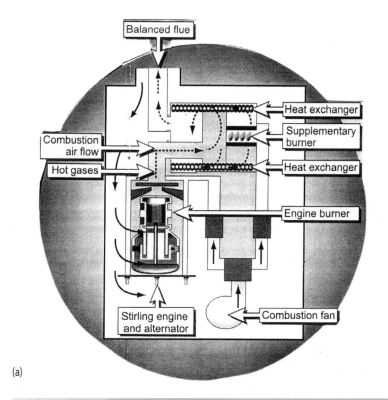

Balanced flue

Heat exchanger

Combustion
air flow

Supplementary
burner

Hot gases

Heat exchanger

Engine burner

Stirling engine
and alternator

Combustion fan

(a)

(b)

for occasions when demand exceeds the output from the engine. The heat is transmitted to the home heating system. There is a supplementary burner in the system for occasions when heat demands exceeds the output from the engine. All models will be able to reduce their heating output to 5kW when necessary. Future models could be adapted to serve warm air heating systems. Multiple unit systems may also be developed to provide increased power and heat.

The Stirling engine is a sealed unit, so the servicing requirements for the Microgen appliance are the same as they would be for a condensing boiler. Another advantage of the system is that it is quiet in operation.

It is expected that pilot units will be installed late 2003/early 2004 and the Microgen appliance should be commercially available late 2004. The cost estimate is that the system will pay back any additional cost over and above any conventional boiler in 4–5 years.

A note of caution. At the moment it is up to a distributed network operator (DNO) whether or not supply from a domestic CHP unit will be accepted by the grid. There is one of a number of anomalies which the government will have to resolve if its enthusiasm for CHP is to be matched by actions. Hopefully the UK will follow the example of other countries and introduce 'net metering'. This means that the meter credits the units generated by the CHP unit at the same rate as the unit cost of power from the grid. Discrepancies in the market across the European Union will be rectified by 2010 by which date the market has to be liberalized. In the meantime, the main benefit of producing on-site electricity is in the avoided cost of importing electricity from the grid at market prices.

Despite the current regulatory problems, the UK Department of Environment Farming and Rural Affairs is optimistic about the prospects for micro-CHP or 'micro-cogeneration', estimating the potential domestic market to be up to 10 million units. With the opening up of the energy markets, micro-CHP is likely to become a major player in the energy stakes, accounting for some 25–30 GW of electricity (GWe). One of the factors favouring this technology is that it can be up to 90 per cent efficient and result in a reduction in total carbon dioxide emissions of up to 50 per cent when compared with the separate production of heat and energy. Large power stations are about 40 per cent efficient. Add to this line losses of 5–7 per cent and it is obvious there is no contest.

In summary, the advantages of micro-CHP or micro-cogeneration are

- It is a robust technology with few moving parts.
- Maintenance is simple (on average once a year).
- Since there is no explosive combustion, the engine produces a noise level equivalent to a refrigerator.
- It is compact with a domestic unit being no larger than an average refrigerator.

- It operates on natural gas, diesel or domestic fuel oil. In the not too distant future machines may be fuelled by biogas from the anaerobic digestion of waste.
- The efficiency is at least 90 per cent compared with 60 per cent for a standard non-condensing boiler.
- Unlike a boiler it produces both heat and electricity, reducing energy use by about 20 per cent and saving perhaps £200–300 on the average annual electricity bill.
- It can be adapted to provide cooling as well as heat.

The UK government is keen to promote this technology and it is always worth checking if grants are available. The best source of advice is the Energy Saving Trust (www.est.org.uk).

Heat pumps

Another cogeneration technology which is predicted to make an impact on the domestic market centres on heat pumps. The advantage of this technology is that it can provide both heating and cooling for the same cost as a conventional central heating system. As the technology is still relatively unknown in the UK it is worth some explanation.

The most efficient is the geothermal heat pump (GHP) which originated in the 1940s and draws its heat from the ground. For this reason it is also called a ground source heat pump. This is another technology which goes back a long way but which is only now realizing its potential as a technology for the future.

Heat pump mechanism

Below a certain depth, say 3 m, the ground maintains a constant temperature of 10–12°C winter or summer. A heat pump extracts some of this warmth and amplifies it to a temperature suitable to supplement space heating (Figure 7.5). There are two major elements in the system:

(1) A high density polyethylene pipe filled with a water and anti-freeze mix buried in the ground causing it to act as a heat transporter. The pipe is laid in a U-configuration either vertically or horizontally. The horizontal type is most common in residential situations where there is usually adequate open space and because it incurs a much lower excavation cost than the alternative.
(2) The heat pump mechanism has the following components:
    An evaporator coil
    A compressor
    A condenser coil
    An expansion valve.

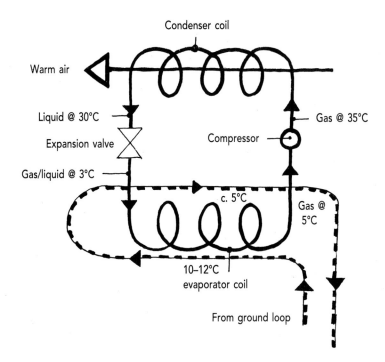

Figure 7.5
Heat pump mechanism.

The operation of the heat pump cycle is:

(1) Liquid refrigerant is forced through an expansion valve.
(2) As the refrigerant leaves the expansion valve it is subject to a loss of pressure.
(3) This causes it to evaporate which, in turn, causes it to remove heat from the water in the ground loop pipes which are wrapped around the evaporator coil.
(4) The water leaving the evaporator casing is cooled ready to pick up more heat from the ground.
(5) The refrigerant is now a gas which next passes through the compressor.
(6) The consequent increase in pressure causes the refrigerant vapour to condense at a fairly high temperature.
(7) As the vapour condenses it releases the heat it absorbed during the evaporation phase which heats up the condenser coil to up to 65°C. At this temperature it provides a useful source of heat to supplement a central heating on domestic hot water system.

Heat pump in cooling mode

A reversing valve enables a heat pump to become a source of cooling in summer. In the cooling mode a GHP is transformed into a refrigerator. Water circulating in the earth loop is warmer than the

Figure 7.6
Ground source heat pump
layout.

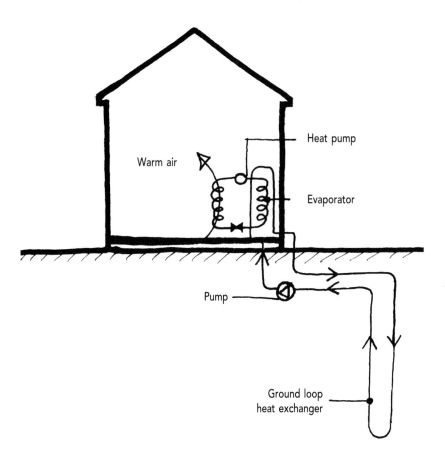

surrounding ground. It therefore releases heat to the ground, cooling in the process. The cooled water then passes through a heat exchanger in the heat pump. Within the heat exchanger, refrigerant gas heated by a compressor releases its heat to the water which then begins its travel to release heat to the ground. The refrigerant having released its heat energy becomes a cold gas after passing through an expansion valve which is used to cool air or water (Figure 7.6).

In a ducted air system, the heat pump's fan circulates warm air from the building over the coils containing the cold refrigerant. The resultant cooled air is then blown through the ductwork of the building. The cold refrigerant in the air coil picks up heat energy from the building and then travels to the compressor where it again becomes a hot gas and the cycle starts again. In passing, it is worth stating that insulation keeps heat out as well as in, so has a cooling value in summer.

The main benefit of this technology is that it uses up to 50 per cent less electricity than conventional electrical heating or cooling. A

GHP uses one unit of electricity to move between three and four units of heat from the earth. This is described as a coefficient of performance (COP) of 3 or 4:1. The theoretical ultimate COP for heat pumps is 14. In the near future a COP of 8 is likely (see Appendix).

Usually the lowest cost option is to use water in a pond, lake or river as the heat transfer medium. Running water is preferable. The supply pipe is run underground from the building and coiled into circles at least 1.75 m below the surface. An architect in Oxford has recently received permission from the Thames Water Authority to use the river for a water source heat pump. This is now in operation at Osney Island. This is an important breakthrough for a technology which is still regarded with suspicion by water authorities fearing, no doubt, that rivers will freeze over (Figure 7.7).

An alternative to ground or water source heat pumps are the air source heat pumps which are becoming increasingly efficient. In fact, milder winters in the UK mean that inverter speed controlled compressors make air source heat pumps more efficient than ground source heat pumps. This version of the heat pump is mainly used to serve ducted air systems. There are very few available which operate wet underfloor heating systems. However, due to the absence of extensive external works, air source heat pumps are much cheaper than ground source systems.

Variations

Rather than using electricity to power the compressor and fans, there is the prospect that natural gas or biofuel could be used to heat a Stirling engine to work the compressor and generate electricity for

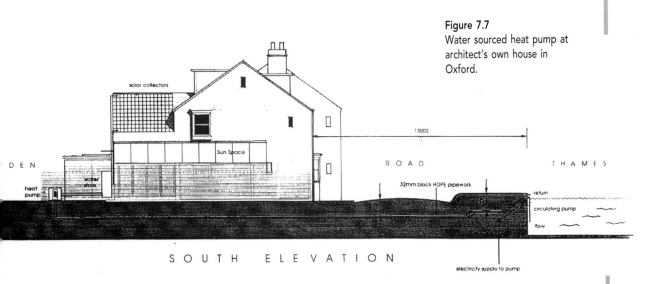

Figure 7.7
Water sourced heat pump at architect's own house in Oxford.

the fans. The excess heat could heat the building or provide domestic hot water.

Another application is in conjunction with heat recovery ventilation (see Chapter 5). The extract air passes through coils containing a liquid refrigerant which picks up the exported heat. On the ventilation side of the system the refrigerant is condensed releasing heat to the interior. The situation can be reversed when the requirement is for cooling.

Economics

In terms of capital cost, it is still the case that heat pumps are at a disadvantage as against fossil fuel technologies. For example, the cost of a ground source heat pump in the UK is at present two to three times that of a conventional fossil fuel boiler. In the case of a resistive electric installation like electric underfloor heating the cost disparity is even greater. It is in running costs that the advantages are to be found. In more recently built well-insulated homes with good thermal mass in the UK it is possible to achieve revenue savings as compared with mains gas, especially when savings in maintenance costs are factored in.

Note. A heat pump was installed in the Millennium House, Building Research Establishment, Garston, Watford. This was the subject of a BBC TV documentary in 1999. The house may be viewed by appointment, Tel. 01923 664400. This was an installation by GeoScience Ltd of Falmouth (www.geoscience.co.uk).

Stop press. The UK Government has now included heat pumps in its range of technologies eligible for grants under the 'Clear Skies' programme.

Evaporative cooling

Most of this book has been concerned with the question of retaining warmth within the home. As stated above, the prediction of climate scientists is that there will be an increased incidence of extremely high temperatures. Already it is known that the year 2002 was the second warmest year on record, so attention will increasingly be focused on cooling.

For several millennia it has been known that evaporating water reduces air temperature in its vicinity. A fountain in the centre of a Roman 'executive' house was not just decorative, it also provided cooling. As hot air hits the cool surface of a pond it causes some evaporation. Heat is transferred from the water to the water vapour causing cooling in the process; the same as the cooling function of evaporating perspiration on the human body. A fountain causes this process to accelerate. So, an open leisure pool in the garden will do more than just provide relaxation, it will also offer relief during extreme heat episodes.

A final note: there is a growing fashion for extending terraces and enlarging patios. It is important to keep hard surfaces to a minimum to limit the extent of run-off for rainwater. If paving slabs are used it is advisable to space them to allow water to drain into the ground. This improves the micro-climate as well as reducing pressure on water treatment plants. Best of all, use recycled slabs.

Fuel cells

Few doubt that the fuel cell will be the ultimate power source of the future and it is already available for the domestic market. So, what is it?

A fuel cell is an electrochemical device that produces electricity in a way that is similar to a battery. But, unlike a battery, it gets its energy from a continuous supply of a fuel – usually hydrogen. It could be conceived as an electrochemical internal combustion engine since the process of creating electricity generates considerable heat. This makes it ideal as a CHP option. Technically it is a reactor which combines hydrogen and oxygen to produce electricity, heat and water. It is a robust technology, quiet in operation, with few moving parts and therefore minimum maintenance requirement and emitting no pollution. The next question is: Where does the hydrogen fuel come from? The answer: from natural gas. Methane is rich in hydrogen which can be extracted by means of a reformer unit. In due course, the electricity needed to split water to release the hydrogen will come from renewable sources, which will make this the ultimate zero pollution power plant.

According to the *New Scientist* (25 November 2000 p. 3), 'Within a couple of years, fuel cells will provide electricity for homes and offices. The source of hydrogen will be natural gas which, if cheap enough, will allow fuel cells to undercut today's combination of heating boiler and mains electricity'. That was a little optimistic as regards the timescale. Nevertheless, International Fuel Cells (US) has been testing a cell producing 5–10 kW of electricity and hot water at 120–160°C for central heating. It plans to be on the market in 2003. In the same year, the US company Plug Power is to market the 'GE HomeGen 7000' domestic fuel cell worldwide.

According to Kevin Kendall, a chemist from the University of Keele, 'Millions of home owners replace their gas-fired central heating systems in Europe every year. Within 5 years they could be installing a fuel cell that would run on natural gas .... Every home could have a combined heat and power plant running off mains gas'. That was said in March 2000, so, only 2 years to go from the time of writing (*New Scientist*, 18 March 2000).

Within the next decade it is predicted there will be a dramatic growth in the use of fuel cells in both static and mobile applications. It may not be a technology for the moment but almost certainly it will come to have a major role in the domestic CHP market.

It has taken since 1839, when Sir William Grove invented the technology, for the fuel cell to be recognized as the likely principle power source of the future. It is the fuel cell that will be the bridge between the hydrocarbon economy and hydrogen-based society. David Hart who is head of fuel cells and hydrogen research at Imperial College has no doubt about the possibilities for fuel cells:

> If fuel cells fulfil their potential, there's no reason why they shouldn't replace almost every battery and combustion engine in the world.
>
> *New Scientist* 'Inside Science, Fuelling the future'
> 16 June 2001.

There is still considerable potential for improvements in the efficiency of fuel cells since they are not dependent upon heat per se, but on electro-chemical conversion, which means they are not limited by the Second Law of Thermodynamics.

In the USA, there is considerable activity in fuel cell development, not least because of the Department of Energy's upbeat stance over the technology. 'The vision is staggering: a society powered almost entirely by hydrogen, the most abundant element in the universe ... The overall goal of the DOE is to replace two to four quads of conventional energy with hydrogen by the year 2010, and replace 10 quads per year by 2030. A quad is the amount of energy consumed by one million households' US NREL.

To explain the operation of a fuel cell the polymer electrolyte membrane fuel cell serves the purpose. Sometimes called the proton exchange membrane fuel cell (PEMFC in either case), it is also referred to as the solid polymer fuel cell. This is one of the most common types of cell being appropriate for both vehicle and static application. Of all the cells in production it has the lowest operating temperature of 80°C. The cell consists of an anode and a cathode separated by an electrolyte, usually teflon. Both the anode and cathode are coated with platinum which acts as a catalyst. Hydrogen is fed to the anode and an oxidant (oxygen from the air) to the cathode. The catalyst on the anode facilitates a reaction causing the hydrogen to split into its constituent protons and electrons. The electrolyte membrane allows only protons to pass through to the cathode, thereby setting up a charge separation in the process. The electrons pass through an external circuit creating useful energy at around 0.7 V, then recombine with protons at the cathode to produce water and heat (Figure 7.8). To build up a useful voltage, cells are stacked between conductive bipolar plates, usually graphite which have integral channels to allow the free flow of hydrogen and oxygen (Figure 7.9).

A variation on this theme is the solid oxide fuel cell. This operates at high temperature, about 800°C. Its great virtue is that it can run on a variety of fuels and its high temperature enables it to break down impurities. It is capable of a wide range of power outputs from 2 to 1000 kW. David Hart believes that, 'solid oxide fuel cells

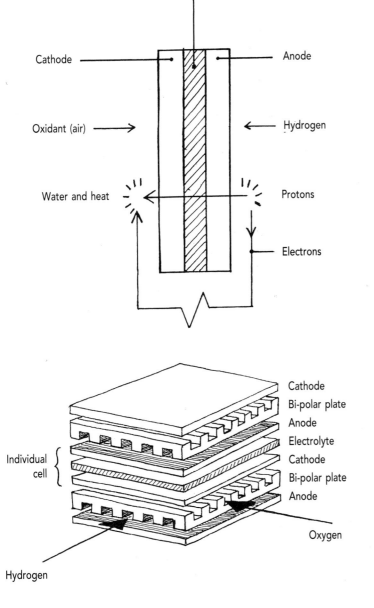

Figure 7.8
Polymer electrolyte or proton exchange membrane fuel cell.

Figure 7.9
Fuel cell stack.

are expected to have the widest range of applications. Large units should be useful in industry for generating electricity and heat. Smaller units could be used in homes ...' (*New Scientist* Inside Science, 'Fuelling the future, 16 June 2001).

Main points

- Alternatives to conventional heating are receiving government support including CHP. BGTechnology's Stirling CHP should be on the market by 2004. Other Stirling systems are currently available including from Powergen.
- Developments in the efficiency of heat pump technology offers the promise of a cost-effective alternative to conventional heating.
- These require specialist installation and expert advice for these technologies can be obtained from the Combined Heat and Power Association and Geoscience for heat pumps.
- Fuel cell technology is progressing in both cost-effectiveness and efficiency. It is almost certainly the prime versatile technology for the medium- to long-term future.

Domestic hot water (DHW)

Chapter Eight

For an average family using between 700 and 1200 litres of hot water per week, the energy involved can be a significant proportion of the whole energy budget at around 20 per cent. If a high level of insulation has been achieved the proportion is higher. The most popular heating method is by an electrical immersion heater because of its convenience, safety and low capital cost. At the same time it is the least environmentally acceptable with a high carbon equivalent for every litre of water. Of all the fossil fuels natural gas or methane creates the least carbon emissions. In terms of kilograms of CO_2 emitted per gigajoule of delivered energy, gas produces 54 kg and electricity 141.6 kg (*Source:* Building Research Establishment).

Most homes have hot water storage cylinders and most are inadequately, if at all, insulated. New cylinders come fitted with an insulation jacket. However, this is usually not up to the advised thickness which should be at least 100 mm. This might be somewhat relaxed if the cylinder is in a closed cupboard used for airing clothes. The efficiency can be significantly increased if heat is recovered from the waste hot water. One way is to employ heat pump technology which was explained in Chapter 7. In the USA and Scandinavia it is becoming increasingly common to exploit the heat recovered from the ventilation system to heat the DHW system. Even in temperate climates there is increasing evidence of solar energy being employed to supplement DHW heating. This will be considered in more detail below.

The alternative to a storage system is the instant point heater. In certain conditions this may be the more economical option. For example, when

- the household consists of one or two persons;
- the number of locations needing hot water is limited;
- simultaneous need for large quantities of hot water is avoided;
- most demand is for small quantities;
- there is no mains gas supply.

This may be a more economical and efficient facility than a storage tank with immersion heater. In small properties it also has the advantage of not requiring a special cupboard.

There is also the option of a gas point heater with a balanced flue. This solves the problem of providing combustion air from the outside whilst eliminating the need for a vertical flue which must have a minimum height to ensure sufficient 'pull' on the waste gases – a potential problem in bungalows. However, there are regulations concerning the positioning of balanced flues particularly in relation to the proximity of opening windows.

Solar thermal energy

It is likely that solar thermal power will provide a major share of the renewable energy needed in the future since solar radiation is by far the largest potential renewable resource. About 1 per cent of the earth's deserts covered with solar thermal plants would have supplied the world's total energy demand for the year 2000.

Energy from the sun serves two energy domains – heat and electricity.

Solar heating

Solar panels have traditionally been associated with providing domestic hot water. Even in temperate climates they offer a useful boost to domestic hot water (DWH) systems. Basically they consist of a circuit of pipes placed on a roof and linked to a DHW cylinder. The most

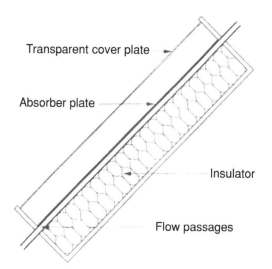

Figure 8.1
Flat plate solar collector.

straightforward type is the flat plate collector. This consists of an array of pipes beneath a matt black metal sheet which absorbs solar heat. This, in turn, is protected by a transparent cover. The underside of the pipes is insulated (Figure 8.1).

This type of collector achieves a temperature of about 35°C which is useful for pre-heating water for a boiler or immersion heater. This is often referred to as 'active solar' due to the fact that the water is pump-driven through the thermal coils. There is an alternative called a thermosyphon system in which circulation of the working fluid is driven by thermal buoyancy. In this case, a storage tank sits at the top of the collector (Figure 8.2).

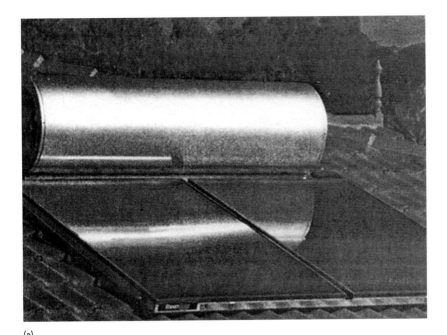

(a)

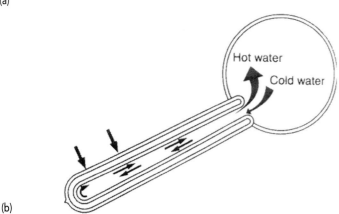

Hot water

Cold water

(b)

Figure 8.2
(a) and (b) Flat plate thermosyphon collector with header tank. *Source*: Courtesy of Renewable Energy World (REW) March–April 2002.

Vacuum tube collectors

In this technology evacuated tubes enclosed within an insulated steel casing work by exploiting the vacuum around the collector. This reduces the heat loss from the system. They can heat water to around 60°C, but sometimes significantly higher. This means that domestic hot water systems may have no need of additional heating. To realize their full potential they should be linked to a storage facility which stores excess warmth in summer to supplement winter heating. This type of solar collector is most efficient in direct solar radiation, but less effective in cloudy or diffuse conditions (Figure 8.3).

There is a further division into direct or 'open loop' systems in which potable water is circulated through the collectors (Figure 8.4) and 'closed loop' or indirect systems which use an anti-freeze heat transfer circulating fluid (Figure 8.5).

It is now possible for the collector system to incorporate a photovoltaic module to provide power for the circulating fan, making it a true zero fossil energy option.

Figure 8.3
Vacuum tube solar collectors on Professor Tony Marmont's Farm, Nottinghamshire.

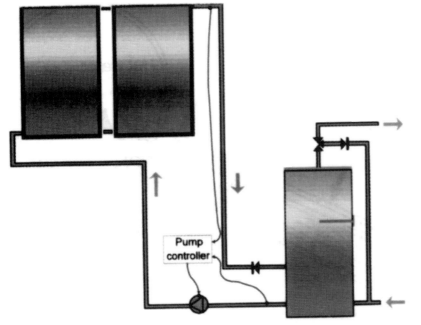

Figure 8.4
Open loop pumped circulation system. Courtesy REW.

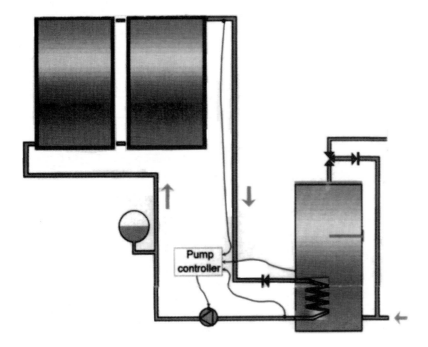

Figure 8.5
Closed loop (indirect) pumped circulation system with internal coil heat exchanger. Courtesy REW.

A type of solar collector which is particularly efficient in cloudy conditions is one which employs 'fin and tube' technology. The effect of this is to increase the surface area of the absorber pipes by 20 per cent. The absorbers are placed behind 3 mm toughened glass with a backing of foil-backed phenolic foam. At an inspection of a 5.2 m² installation of this system by the author in January 2003, the air

Figure 8.6
Sunuser solar thermal panel.

Figure 8.7
Sunuser retrofitted solar thermal collectors.

temperature was 6°C and the sky cloudy and dull. The temperature of the water fed from the panels was 21°C. Whilst not exactly warm, this gives an indication of the rate of temperature gain. In this property the space heating is provided by warm air, so the solar collectors are dedicated to providing domestic hot water. Since they were installed the immersion heater has been switched off. The area of the house is approximately 250 m² occupied by two adults. The overall cost of the installation including VAT, was £5103.00 (Figures 8.6, 8.7 and 8.8).

Figure 8.8
Sunuser cylinder and controls.

In more conventional homes with wet central heating systems there are two options: a dual coil system or a twin tank arrangement. The first system allows water to be drawn from the taps with surplus replenishing the hot water cylinder.

With the dual coil arrangement (Figure 8.9) the existing central heating or boiler pipe work is relocated to the upper part of the cylinder, while the solar heated water enters at the lower part. A temperature differential controller measures the difference between the solar panels and the cylinder and activates a pump whenever the temperature in the collectors is greater than that in the cylinder (Figure 8.10). This system is designed and manufactured by Sunuser Ltd, Leeds, UK; Tel: 0113 262 0261; E-mail: solar@sunuser.co.uk

In Europe, there are wide variations in the application of active solar heating. For example, Austria has almost 18 m^2 per 1000 inhabitants of installed capacity compared with the UK which boasts about 0.2 m^2. Yet the UK climate is not all that different from that of Austria. There is a big opportunity gap.

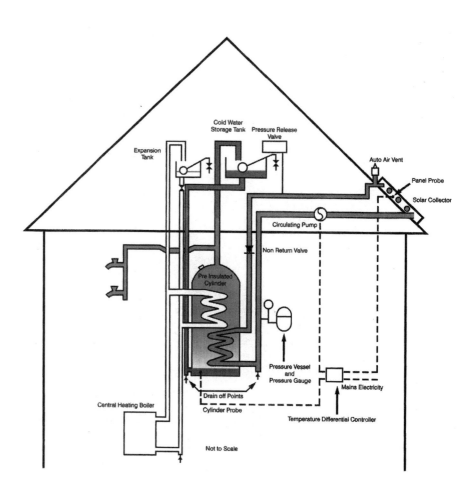

Figure 8.9
Sunuser dual coil system.

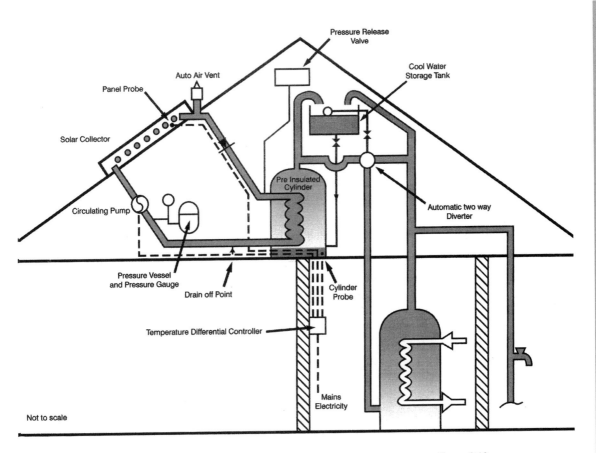

Figure 8.10
Sunuser twin tank system.

Solar thermal hybrids

In most instances in the UK climate it would be necessary to have backup heat for the hot water system. Usually this is provided by an electric immersion heater. However, lower running costs can be realized with a solar–gas combination cylinder. The principle here is that a 240 litre tank is heated by flat plate solar collectors supplemented by a gas burner within the body of the cylinder. It provides space heating and domestic hot water. A heat exchanger coil in the upper half of the tank heats the central heating circuit. A production solar–gas combination boiler with 2.83 m² of solar collector produces 4 GJ/year; a 5.4 m² collector supplies 5.64 GJ/year. A test involving 25 units showed a boiler efficiency of 90.1 per cent. On average, consumers saved 650 m³ of natural gas compared with their former systems. Based on the current price of gas (1999), the payback time is 13 years. However, gas prices are rising. The other factor to consider is that the system would be almost zero carbon if at some future date it employed biogas (Figure 8.11)

Flat bed solar collector

(1) Absorber
(2) 40 mm insulation plate, CFC-free
(3) Low-iron tempered glass
(4) Temperature sensor in the collector
(5) Aluminium rim

Cylinder

(1) Pump
(2) Delta temperature control
(3) Supply tap
(4) Temperature sensor in the boiler
(5) Gas burner
(6) Central heating coil
(7) Hot and cold water pipes
(8) Level tap
(9) Maximum flow restrictor
(10) Intake combination
(11) Thermostat control for boiler
(12) Boiler insulation material, CFC-free
(13) Outside temperature control
(14) Central heating pump
(15) Radiator
(16) Maximum pressure valve

Figure 8.11
Solar–gas combination cylinder.

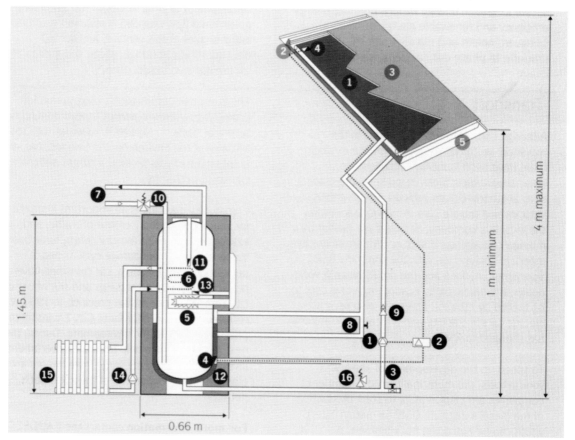

Economics

Unfortunately, while this technology is one of the cheapest renewable options it is still not cost-effective weighed against fossil-based energy, with a pay-back time of around 20 years. However, this cost-effectiveness can be considerably improved if complete roof renovation is being undertaken and the flat bed collectors integrated into the new roof. The reality is that the market will only grow significantly at this stage if:

- There is direct or indirect government support for the technology;
- Following this intervention, the market expands to achieve economies of scale;
- The product is of the highest quality and fitting procedures simplified and standardized;
- There is an adequate network of trained and accredited specialist installers.

Main points

- Hot water cylinders should have at least 100 mm of insulation.
- One- or two-person households may find it more economical to use point heaters for DHW.
- Gas is more cost-effective than electricity for DHW heating.
- Solar thermal collectors can significantly boost DHW, though they are still some way from being cost-effective.
- In the UK, solar collectors should be tilted in a southerly direction with virtually no overshading. Certain types are particularly appropriate for the cloudy conditions so common in this climate.

Chapter Nine

Lighting

The first objective should be to make the best possible use of daylight. External obstructions, heavy net curtains or curtains which, when open, fall within the boundary of the window, can all cause lights to be switched on sooner than necessary. It is often the case that the desire for privacy conflicts with energy-saving imperatives.

Light coloured internal surfaces maximize light reflection. The obsession of the architects of the Modern Movement with light led to the fashion for white, uncluttered interior walls. This reduced dependency on artificial light.

Internal spaces like some bathrooms obviously need artificial light and the same is frequently true of hallways and staircases. One answer is the light pipe. This consists of a tube which is mirrored on its inner surface. A domed rooflight is fitted over the top of the tube and a light diffuser at the bottom. Daylight or sunlight are guided down the tube, reflected by the mirrored surface. Such a device transmits a surprising amount of illumination (Figure 9.1).

Artificial light

Artificial lighting in homes is often inefficient and wasteful. Aesthetic considerations tend to outweigh practicality and economy. For example, we often perform close-up tasks, such as reading or sewing, using the overall light in a room rather than employing appropriate task lighting. This involves eye strain leading to subliminal stress resulting in headaches and ultimately the possibility of eyesight damage. So, this section considers:

- The design of a lighting layout;
- The appropriate types of lamp.

Design for efficiency and comfort

At the outset, it is worth describing the terms used in lighting. There are three basic measures:

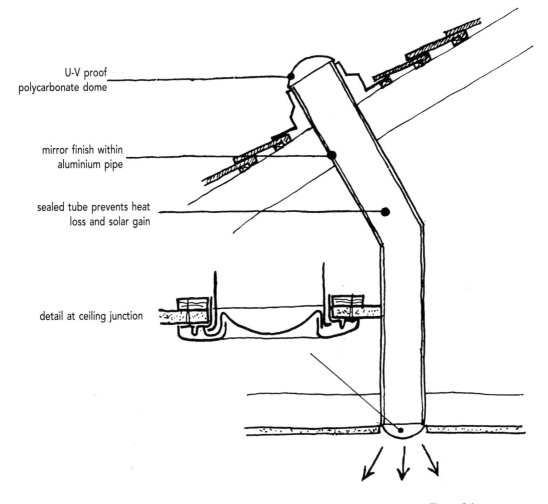

U-V proof
polycarbonate dome

mirror finish within
aluminium pipe

sealed tube prevents heat
loss and solar gain

detail at ceiling junction

Figure 9.1
Light pipe diagram.

- The output of a lamp in terms of its level of illumination is denoted by lumens (lm);
- The level of illumination required in a given space is defined as lux (lx);
- The performance of a particular lamp is described as its 'lamp efficacy'. The greater the luminous efficacy the better the lamp at converting electricity into light.

Background illumination in a living room should be around 300 lx. A popular means of achieving this is by up-lighters which reflect off a white ceiling, giving a soft, overall light. Point light sources create glare, increasing the contrast between the light source and the background. The eye adjusts to the bright light by reducing the pupil size, making the surroundings even more gloomy. As an aside, it is worth pointing out that a television is a bright light source.

The area surrounding the TV should be at the recommended background level to avoid eye strain which is exacerbated by rapidly moving images. The same applies to computers. Wherever possible background light should be from a reflected source. For circulation spaces, the recommended level is 200 lx.

For task lighting the recommended level is at least 500 lx over an area defined by the task in question.

Types of lamp

Most households still rely on the traditional incandescent tungsten filament lamp. As the name suggests, it generates a great deal of heat. In fact it produces 95 per cent heat at 2000°C within the lamp and 5 per cent light. Consequently it has poor efficacy amounting to 13 lm/W. Life expectancy is around 1000 hours. A slight improvement is achieved by a variation of the type known as tungsten halogen lamps. These are compact units generating a bright point light which makes them popular for task lighting. Their efficacy is raised to 17 lm/W and they have an improved life expectancy of 2000–4000 hours, depending on the model.

For most situations, incandescent lamps should be replaced by compact fluorescent lamps (CFLs). These are a development from the conventional fluorescent tube. These tubes have been shrunk and coiled so they are only marginally larger than a tungsten bulb. They have electronic ballasts which enables them to oscillate at 20 000 cycles per second – way beyond the power of the eye to detect. The old fluorescents oscillated at 50 cycles per second, which made them a major culprit for inducing 'sick building syndrome', probably due to the fact that the flicker rate was subliminally perceived. A 15 W CFL is equivalent to a 60 W incandescent bulb. The spectral output is similar whilst it uses only 25 per cent of the energy. Another bonus is that a CFL lasts around 7500 hours.

It is also possible to use dimming controls on CFLs, whereby the electrical consumption is directly proportional to the intensity of light.

CFLs are more expensive than tungsten bulbs, but this is soon offset by the energy savings and longer life. These gains are more marginal for spaces that are used intermittently for short periods, such as store rooms and bathrooms.

Most efficient of all is the latest fluorescent tube called the T5. It is a 15-mm diameter tube with a luminous efficacy of 106 lm/W.

The future

Semi-conductor technology could be about to invade the sphere of lighting in the form of the light emitting diode (LED). The principle is that a small electrical current applied to a diode made from a semi-conductor material raises electrons to a higher energy state. The result is the production of photons (particles of light) in the visible spectrum. Up to the present it has not been possible to produce pure white light from an LED. When this breakthrough occurs we can expect a revolution in lighting. LEDs produce 100 lm/W and have a life span of up to 100 000 hours. Furthermore, they are a fraction of the size of existing lamps and will be available in a range of colours.

Main points

- Make maximum use of natural light with light coloured wall and ceiling surfaces.
- Light pipes are a useful means of directing daylight to internal spaces, such as bathrooms and toilets.
- With artificial lighting it is important to create the right balance between background and task lighting.
- Glare induces stress.
- For background lighting an indirect source, e.g. reflected off the ceiling, avoids glare.
- In most situations compact fluorescent lamps (CFLs) should replace incandescent bulbs.

Chapter Ten

The home as micro-power station

We have already noted how CHP units provide both heat and electricity. The next matter to be considered is whether it is worthwhile installing systems which solely produce electricity, often called 'embedded generation'. For the individual home, the most common technology for this purpose is photovoltaic cells (PVs). Under present regulations in the UK and at current electricity prices this is not a cost-effective investment, despite the fact that government subsidies to offset the capital cost may be available. However, situations can change quite rapidly for several reasons:

- The unit cost of PV cells is likely to fall significantly in the near future.
- The European Union will be regularizing the electricity market in due course, ensuring that small generators receive a reasonable return for their investment. (In Germany, it is a profitable investment thanks to the Renewable Energy Law.)
- There will be increasing international pressure to reduce carbon dioxide emissions. The UK had made a commitment to reduce its emissions by 20 per cent by 2010 against 1990 levels. It has just been abandoned at the time of writing, no doubt because it would only be possible with a really ambitious programme of renewable energy.
- There is strong political and economic pressure to embrace the principle of distributed generation.

The final point calls for an explanation. Distributed generation means drawing electricity from a wide range of small power plants, down to the size of an individual home with PVs, CHP or a wind generator. Under the present arrangement, the national grid obtains its electricity from a small number of large power stations which then distribute the power over considerable distances. As stated earlier, this is a system which can be as low as 35 per cent efficient when line losses are taken into account. It is also vulnerable to failure due to severe weather. In the winter at the end of 2002, storm damage left some communities without power for weeks.

The US energy expert Carl J Weinberg affirms that 'the conceptual model of a utility as large central power plants connected to customers by wires may well not be the model for the future'. This theme was taken up by the Royal Commission on Environmental Pollution which recommends, 'a shift from large all-electricity plant towards more numerous combined heat and power plants. The electricity system will have to undergo major changes to cope with this development and the expansion of smaller scale renewable energy sources' (22nd Report, *Energy, The Changing Climate*, (2000), p. 169).

Developments in information technology are the key to this energy transformation. It is now capable of managing the complexities of a system with a large number of distributed electricity producers without centralized control. It can deal with the interplay of supply and demand providing hour by hour the most equitable price balance between consumers and generators, however small they may be.

Photovoltaic cells (PVs)

PVs are devices which convert light directly into electricity. At present, most PVs consist of two thin layers of a semi-conducting material, each layer having different electrical characteristics. In most common PV cells both layers are made from silicon but with different, finely calculated amounts of impurities: p-type and n-type. The introduction of impurities is known as 'doping'. As a result of the doping, one layer of silicon is negatively charged (n-type) and has a surplus of electrons. The other layer is given a positive side (p-type) and an electron deficit. When light falls on a PV cell electrons are forced from one side to the other due to the radiative energy from the sun. Some of the electrons are captured as useful energy and directed to an external circuit (Figure 10.1).

Cells with different characteristics and efficiencies can be created by using different base and doping materials. The output is direct current (DC) which must be changed to alternating current (AC) by means of an inverter if it is to be fed to the grid. Converting to AC current involves a power loss. The Oxford University Environmental Change Institute compared two types of inverter. The one which operated better in the cloudy conditions of the UK was NKF OK4E. Achieving high efficiencies at low input power levels is an important feature of an inverter in the UK. Another device is required to ensure that the current is grid compatible which means 240 V at 50 Hz.

The capacity of cells to convert light into electricity is defined by Watts peak (Wp). This is based on a bench test and is the power generated by a PV under light intensity of 1000 W/m^2, equivalent to bright sun. The efficiency of a cell is a function of both peak output and area. This is a laboratory measurement and does not necessarily give a true indication of energy yield.

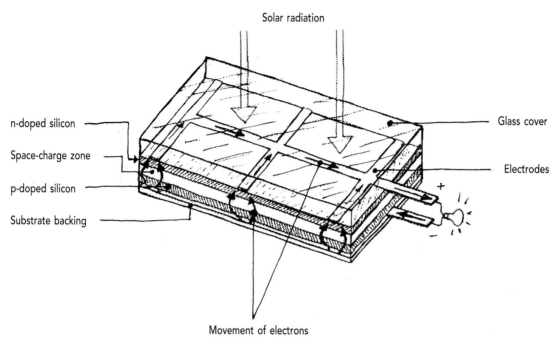

n-doped silicon

Space-charge zone

p-doped silicon

Substrate backing

Solar radiation

Glass cover

Electrodes

Movement of electrons

Figure 10.1
Photovoltaic cell structure and function.

Monocrystalline silicon

At the time of writing, the most efficient PVs are monocrystalline silicon consisting of wafers of a pure crystal of silicon. They achieve a peak output of about 15 per cent. That means that 15 per cent of daylight is converted to electricity when daylight is at its maximum intensity. Due to the production processes involved these cells are expensive.

The solar cell size of around 10 × 10 cm has a peak output of about 1.5 W. To realize a usable amount of electricity cells are wired into modules which, in turn, are electrically connected to form a string. One or more strings form an array of modules.

The cells are sandwiched between an upper layer of toughened glass and a bottom layer of various materials, including glass, Tedlar or aluminium. It must be remembered that a number of linked cells produces a significant amount of current therefore during installation solar cells should be covered, whilst all the electrical connections are made.

Multicrystalline silicon

In the production process of this cell, molten silicon is cast in blocks containing random crystals of silicon. In appearance cells are blue and square. It is cheaper than a monocrystalline cell but has a lower efficiency ranging between 8 and 12 per cent.

A variation of silicon technology has been developed by Spheral Solar of Cambridge, Ontario. It has produced a flexible panel made of minute silicon beads sandwiched between two thin layers of aluminium foil sealed on both sides with plastic. Each bead converts sunlight into electricity with an efficiency of 11 per cent. It is much lighter than PVs currently available and can be shaped to follow almost any profile. It holds the promise of being an ideal retrofit PV panel for existing roofs. Commercial production is due to start in 2004 (*New Scientist* 15 February 2003. p. 19).

Amorphous silicon

This cell does not have a crystalline structure, but is stretched into thin layers which can be deposited on a backing material, which can be rigid or flexible. It is the first of a new breed of PVs based on thin film technology. By building up layers tuned to different parts of the solar spectrum known as a double or triple junction cell, a peak efficiency of 6 per cent is achievable. Unlike the crystalline cells, it is capable of bulk production and is therefore potentially cheaper.

Cadmium telluride (CdTe) and copper indium diselenide (CIS)

These cells are a further development of thin film technology, having efficiencies of about 7 and 9 per cent, respectively. At present, prices are comparatively high but will reduce as volume of sales increases.

In summary, costs range between £2 and £4 per Wp. However, unit cost is not necessarily the only criterion. Different cells have varying optimum conditions which have been highlighted by a research programme recently completed by the Oxford University Environmental Change Institute. This showed that the amount of electricity generated by a PV array rated at 1 kWp in 1 year varies considerably between different technologies. For example, CIS (Seimens ST 40) gave the best returns at over 1000 kWh per kWp per year in the UK. Double junction amorphous silicon cells were close behind. This is because these cells are more effective in the cloudy conditions so prevalent in the UK. Single junction amorphous silicon cells were the poorest performers. The best performing modules produced nearly twice as much power as the lowest yielding cells, so it is very much a case of 'buyer beware'.

A sloping roof facing a southerly direction is the ideal situation, provided it is not overshadowed by trees or other buildings. However, east and west orientations can produce significant amounts of electricity. The optimum angle of tilt depends on latitude. In London, it is 35°. As a rough guide, in London 1 m^2 of monocrystalline PVs could produce 111 kilowatt hours of electricity per year. On low pitch or flat roofs it is advisable to mount the cells on tilt structures at the correct orientation. However, in the UK climate, a flat roof can still deliver 90 per cent of the optimum output.

Standard PV modules can easily be fixed to an existing roof. However, if a roof covering needs to be replaced, it then could become a cost-effective option to use solar slates, tiles or shingles to maintain a traditional appearance. The range of options offered by Solar Century is a useful indication of the possibilities available to the homeowner. A sample of their specifications is given in full, courtesy of Solar Century.

Solar shingles

Ideally suited to the UK climate, solar shingles use triple junction technology to produce electricity even on cloudy days (Figure 10.2).

Power, 17 Wp per tile
Efficiency, 6–7 per cent
Product size, Active area 138 × 2136 mm
Product weight, 6.9 kg/m^2
Power per module, 17 W
Area per kWp, approximately 18 m^2
Modules per m^2, 3.26
Exposed area, width 2195 mm ± 6 mm, height 305 mm
Total active area, 0.30 m^2

Features

- Truly integrated solar PV roofing product
- Low visual impact
- Avoids planning difficulties
- No glass, therefore durable, no UV absorption
- Lightweight
- Easy to lay
- Low embodied energy
- Replaces existing tiles
- Self cleaning
  - Triple junction means: works under low light conditions; more delivered power per peak Watt; better temperature coefficient; good for diffuse skies.
  - Under temperate climate conditions a yield of about 860 to 950 kWh/kWp/year is possible. This figure is 10 to 20 per cent better than poly-crystalline PV.
- By-pass diode in every cell gives superior shading tolerance.
- 20 year warranty

(a)

Figure 10.2
(a, b) Solar shingles.

(b)

Sunslates

Individual slates that are fitted with high efficiency solar cells, designed to look and perform just like your normal roof slates. They are extremely versatile and are quick and easy to install, providing clean electricity all year round.

Sunslates® are suitable for any roofing situation where a conventional tile can be used and are installed on to the building just like normal roof tiles. The tiles fit to standard slate battens and the easy slate-to-slate connectors mean that installation is quick and easy, with no structural alterations required (Figure 10.3).

Figure 10.3
Sunslates.

Efficiency, 10 per cent
kWh per kWp (south facing at 30°), 750
Area per kWp, 10 m^2
Actual size, 720 × 480 mm
Exposed size, 300 × 480 mm
Number and size of cells, 6 × 125 × 125 mm
Installed weight, 35.8 kg/m^2

Features

- Sunslates are roof integrated, i.e. take the place of traditional roof tiles, so they fit seamlessly into the building design of any shaped roof.
- The systems have a good power output even in low light conditions, this means that they perform well, even in the unpredictable UK climate.
- Individual Sunslate connection sockets containing by-pass diodes enable the roof to generate electricity even if a tile is partly shaded.
- Sunslates are designed to blend in with the surrounding tiles, as well as the environment, so planning permission is only required in some conservation areas or on grade one listed properties.
- The tiles are fitted to the roof with standard storm hooks, providing just as much protection from high winds as traditional tiles.
- The tempered glass covering adds to the tile's durability and their ability to withstand the rigours of the tough UK climate.

Glass laminates

Solar glass laminates are attractive and unusual, and provide electricity and insulation. They are available in a wide range of colours (Figure 10.4).

Glass laminates form the conservatory roof in the 'Orange At Home' house of the future. The glass used is very high quality and heat-strengthened. A resin layer is included to make them shatter-resistant. This also has the effect of making the laminates insulating, acting like double glazing. The solar cells within the laminates have the beneficial side effect of reducing glare. Solar glass laminates are made to order, to your specifications. You can decide on the colours, type of glass and how much light you want to let through.

Sunstation

These are retrofit modules that are fitted to the property's original roof. A simple, cost-effective solar electric solution for the home. The

Figure 10.4
(a, b) Glass laminates.

(a)

(b)

Figure 10.5
(a, b) Sunstation.

(a)

(b)

Sunstation® is versatile and easy to install. It is an all-inclusive system, so no hidden costs or hassles. In most cases Solar Century can install your Sunstation® in just 1 day. The Sunstation® is modular and comes in different system sizes, enabling you to mix and match to suit your requirements and your budget (Figure 10.5).

Sunstation® 8 panel
System size, 0.96 kWp
Electricity, 750k Wh
CO_2, 585 kg
Area, 7.8 m^2
Weight, 121.2 kg

Sunstation® 12 panel
System size, 1.44 kWp
Electricity, 1100 kWh
CO_2, 770 kg
Area, 11.7 m^2
Weight, 176.8 kg

To maximize the contribution of a south-facing sloping roof, it would also be useful to install flat bed solar thermal collectors integrated with PV modules (Figure 10.6).

Prospects for PVs in the developed countries

The European Photovoltaic Industry Association (EPIA) has made predictions about the penetration of PVs into the energy market by 2020. Worldwide PVs should be generating about 274 Terra Watt hours (TWh), which would be enough to meet 30 per cent of the electricity needs of the whole of Africa. Installed capacity would be 195 GWp of which half would be grid-connected in the industrialized countries. It is reckoned that about 80 per cent of the capacity in developed countries will be situated on residential buildings. That works out at 35 million people in Europe alone on the assumption that the average PV output for an individual home is 3 kWp serving three people. This amounts to nothing less than a revolution in the way electricity will be generated, offering considerable cash savings to householders and massive reductions in CO_2 emissions. At today's prices a PV module should, by then, cost about 1 Euro (US $1 or UK 70p) per Wattp. By 2040 the solar contribution is likely to reach 21 per cent of the world's electricity output.

If these predictions are anywhere near the mark, it means that the unit cost of PV modules will fall substantially due both to technological improvements and economies of scale. Cells coated with light-sensitive dyes are close to market-ready and are expected to be one

(a)

Figure 10.6
Solar house, Freiburg showing
PVs and solar flat bed thermal
collector with header tank.

(b)

quarter the price of the current technology. In addition, solar cells have been produced in the laboratory which deliver a peak efficiency of 31 per cent, so we can expect significant improvements in the technology in the near future.

Note: at the time of writing grants of up to 50 per cent of the installation cost are available from the Energy Saving Trust (www.est.org.uk/solar).

Wind power

The home may not seem an obvious location for a wind generator. The public perception is of large 'windmill' rotors set in the landscape or off-shore. However, there is increasing interest in the development of small-scale or micro-wind generators suitable for attachment to buildings.

In this context 'small' means wind machines that are scaled from a few Watts to 20 kW. Machines between 1 and 5 kW may be used to provide either direct current or alternating current. They are mainly confined to the domestic level and are often used to charge batteries. The larger machines are more appropriate for groups of houses. As an example, the Hockerton Zero Energy Housing Project in Nottinghamshire has recently installed a 5 kW horizontal axis turbine rated at 270 V three phase, serving five homes. It is expected to generate 11 652 kWh per year. The height is 26 m and blade diameter 5.6 m. It exports excess load to the grid which will ultimately become profitable. The cost of the equipment was £19 300. The total cost including installation came to £26 142, including VAT at 5 per cent.

The supplier was Proven Engineering Ltd (www. proven-energy.com).

This scale of horizontal axis turbine is feasible where a group of homes can be recruited to join together to share the costs and benefits of wind power. It is also appropriate for homes in rural situations (Figures 10.7 and 10.8).

As stated earlier, small-scale electricity production on site has economic disadvantages in the UK given the present impediments to small-scale intermittent generation. Currently, the government is considering how to redress this inequity and thereby give a substantial boost to the market for small-scale renewables. Wind generation will do well if this happens, since it is at present usually less expensive in terms of installed cost per kilowatt than PV which makes it an attractive proposition as a building integrated power source.

Wind patterns in the built environment are complex as the air passes over, around and between buildings. Accordingly a wind generator introduced into this environment must be able to cope with

Figure 10.7
Wind turbine, Hockerton
Housing Project.

high turbulence caused by buildings. Such conditions tend to favour vertical axis machines as opposed to the horizontal versions which have proliferated in wind farms. This is because the vertical versions may be able to operate at lower wind speeds and they are less stressed mechanically by turbulence.

By their very nature the vertical axis machines are not affected by changes in wind direction or turbulence. They can be sited on roofs or walls. They have been successful when mounted on the sides of oil platforms in the North Sea (Figure 10.9).

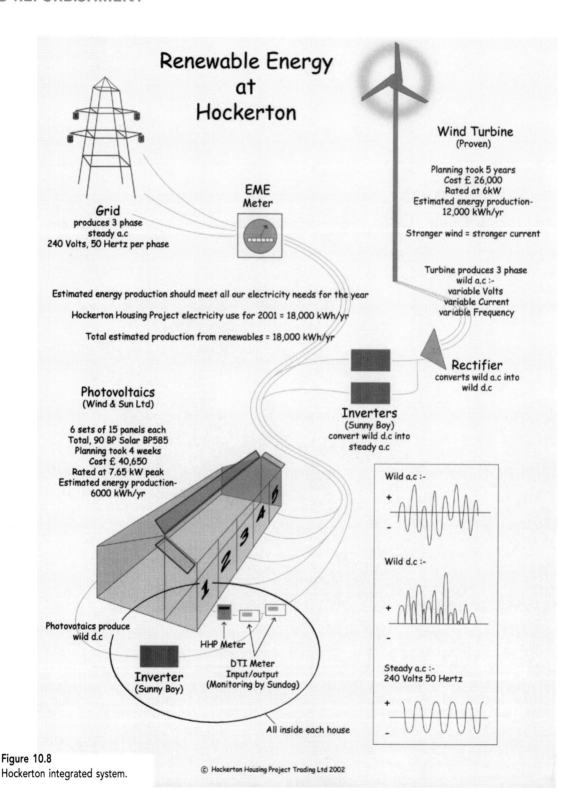

Figure 10.8
Hockerton integrated system.

© Hockerton Housing Project Trading Ltd 2002

Figure 10.9
Helical side-mounted turbine on oil platform.

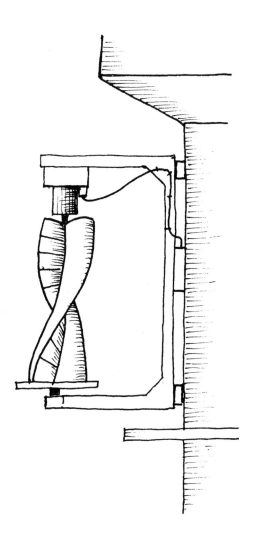

The machines are well balanced, transmitting low levels of vibration and bending stress to walls or roofs. They also have a high output power to weight ratio.

An estimate in 'WIND Directions' March 2001 suggests that the global market for small turbines by 2005 will be around Euros 173 million and several hundreds of million by 2010. For example, in the Netherlands alone there is the potential for 20 000 urban turbines to be installed on industrial and commercial buildings by 2011.

Currently there are several versions of vertical axis machines on the market. When it is fully appreciated that these machines are reliable, almost silent, low maintenance, easy to install and competitive on price, it is likely the market will expand rapidly. At present the regulatory regime for small turbines is much less onerous than for >20 kW machines.

Development work is continuing on designs for turbines which are suitable for the difficult wind conditions found in urban situations. This is appropriate since climate change predictions indicate that wind speeds will increase as the atmosphere heats up and so becomes more dynamic. There is growing confidence that there will be a large market for mini-turbines in various configurations on offices, housing blocks and individual dwellings.

Types of small-scale wind turbine

Most small systems have a direct drive permanent magnet generator which limits mechanical transmission losses. Systems under 2 kW usually have a 24–48 V capacity aimed at battery charging or a DC circuit rather than having grid compatibility.

As stated earlier, vertical axis turbines are particularly suited to urban situations and to being integrated into buildings. They are discrete and virtually silent and much less likely to trigger the wrath of planning officials.

A problem with some very small vertical axis machines is that they need mechanical start-up which can be achieved either by an electric motor or a link to a Savonius type rotor. The most common vertical axis machine is the helical turbine as seen at the Earth Centre, Doncaster (Figure 10.10). In that instance it is mounted on a tower, but it can also be side-hung on a building as shown earlier.

Another variety is the S-Rotor which has an S-shaped blade (Figure 10.11). The Darrieus-Rotor employs three slender eliptical blades which can be assisted by a wind deflector. This is an elegant machine which nevertheless needs start-up assistance. A variation of the genre is the H-Darrieus-Rotor with triple vertical blades extending from the central axis. Yet another configuration is the Lange turbine which has three sail-like wind scoops. Last in this group is the 'Spiral flugel' turbine, in which twin blades create, as the name indicates, a spiral partnership (Figure 10.12).

There is increasing interest in the way that the design of buildings can incorporate renewable technologies, including wind turbines. Up to now, such machines have been regarded as adjuncts to buildings, but a concept patented by Altechnica of Milton Keynes demonstrates how multiple turbines can become a feature of the design.

The system is designed to be mounted on the ridge of a roof or at the apex of a curved roof section. Rotors are incorporated in a cage-like structure which is capped with an aerofoil wind concentrator called in this case a 'Solairfoil'. The flat top of the solairfoil can accommodate PVs (Figure 10.13).

The advantage of this system is that it does not become an over-assertive visual feature and is perceived as an integral design element. It is also a system which can easily be fitted to existing buildings where the wind regime is appropriate. It can accommodate

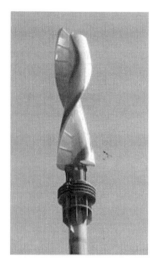

Figure 10.10
Helical turbine on a column at the Earth Centre, Doncaster.

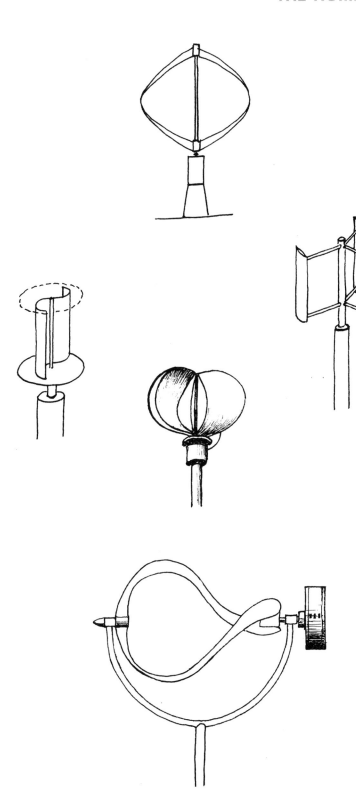

Figure 10.11
Left: S-Rotor; top centre:
Darrieus-Rotor; bottom centre:
Lange turbine; right: H-
Darrieus-Rotor.

Figure 10.12
Spiral Flugel rotor.

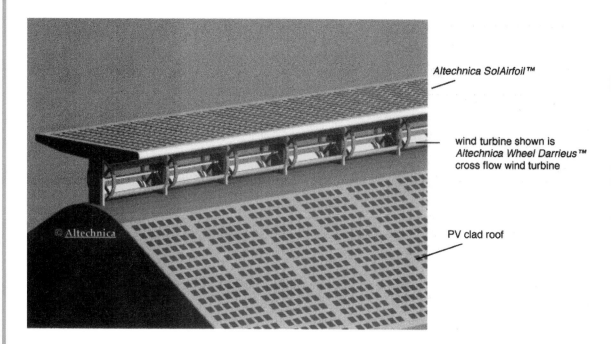

Altechnica SolAirfoil™

wind turbine shown is
Altechnica Wheel Darrieus™
cross flow wind turbine

PV clad roof

© Altechnica

Figure 10.13
'Aeolian' roof devised by
Altechnica.

vertical or horizontal axis turbines according to the characteristics of the site. It is a method of discretely capturing the elements whilst also offering a platform for PVs. The wind generators continue operating at night when PVs are in retirement.

It may be necessary to check if planning permission is necessary and possibly Building Regulations approval for its structural integrity.

Research conducted by Delft University and Ecofys in The Netherlands suggests that low rise, suburban domestic buildings will be subject to significant turbulence and changes in wind direction. The prediction from climate scientists is that these conditions will intensify as global warming gathers pace. This indicates that vertical axis turbines could be the most suitable for most homes.

If the preferred option is for a horizontal axis turbine, as at Hockerton, then it is important to check the wind patterns around the house for at least 3 months in advance. If there are no major obstructions to wind access, then the turbine should be at least 6 m above any obstruction within a radius of 150 m. If possible the plant should be sited within 30 m of the property to limit line losses.

For further information refer to Smith (2002) and the British Wind Energy Association (www.bwea.com).

Grants

In January 2003, the UK energy minister announced the 'Clear Skies' initiative. This is a capital grants programme aimed at communities and individual householders. Grants will be available for residents in England, Wales and Northern Ireland with a parallel scheme being operated in Scotland. Systems must be installed by an accredited installer. Further information from: www.clear-skies.org; Clear Skies hotline: 0870 2430930.

Homeowners can also apply for capital grants for the installation of PVs under the first phase of the Major Photovoltaics Demonstration Programme which aims at assisting with the installation of PVs in 3000 homes. Information from: www.solarpvgrants.co.uk; Helpline: 0800 298 3978.

It was stated in the text that small electricity suppliers would, at present, find it difficult to receive payment for exports to the grid. In the case of a wind generator serving several houses, it may be possible to qualify for Renewables Obligation Certificate, which entitles the holder to receive payment from an electricity distributor for contributions to the grid which exceed 500 kWh per month. The actual requirement is for 1 MW, but any amount over 500 kWh is counted as 1 MW for accountancy purposes. At present, all electricity distributors called District Network Operators (DNOs) are obliged to take a percentage of their electricity from renewable sources. At the moment they are having difficulty meeting that obligation and therefore would welcome imports from small generators. For further information contact the Regulator Ofgen, web address: www.ofgen.gov.uk/newprojects

Main points

- The UK Government is warming to the idea of distributed generation.
- This could, in due course, make generating electricity in the home an attractive proposition.
- The two most viable technologies at present are PVs and wind.
- If considering either option, first consult the specialists, for example Solar Century for PVs and Proven Engineering for small-scale wind generators.
- Vertical axis wind turbines are, in most circumstances, the more appropriate for attachment to buildings.
- PVs function best with a southerly orientation without overshading.
- If considering any form of on site electricity generation, first consult the planners and then a district network operator, if the intention is to feed into the grid.

Chapter Eleven Water and energy conservation in appliances

Not only is water a precious resource in its own right, there is also an energy component in storing and transporting it and making it drinkable. On average, a person in the UK uses 135 litres (30 gallons) of water per day. Of this total about half is used flushing toilets and for personal hygiene. A really thorough home ecological improvement strategy should have three components:

- Reduce consumption;
- Harvest rainwater;
- Recycle grey water.

Reducing consumption

Flushing toilets use about 30 per cent of total household consumption. This can be reduced by changing to a low flush toilet (2–4 litres) or a dual flush cistern. Aerating (spray) taps on basins, sinks and on shower heads make a big impact on consumption. All appliances should have isolating stop cocks so that the whole system does not have to be drained off if one item has a problem. Washing machines and dish washers vary in the amount of water they consume. This is one of the factors which should influence the choice of white goods which will be considered later in this chapter.

On average, about 200 litres of rainwater fall on the roof of a 100-m^2 house each day in the UK. In many homes this is collected in water butts and used to irrigate the garden. However, it has wider uses. There are several proprietary systems for collecting and treating rainwater so that it can be used to flush WCs and for clothes washing machines. An example is the Vortex water harvesting system which serves roof areas up to 200 m^2 and 500 m^2, respectively. Recycled rainwater must only be sourced from roofs. Storage tanks are either concrete or glass-reinforced plastic (GRP). There are controls to ensure that mains water can make good any deficiencies in rainfall. If filtered rainwater is to be used for other domestic

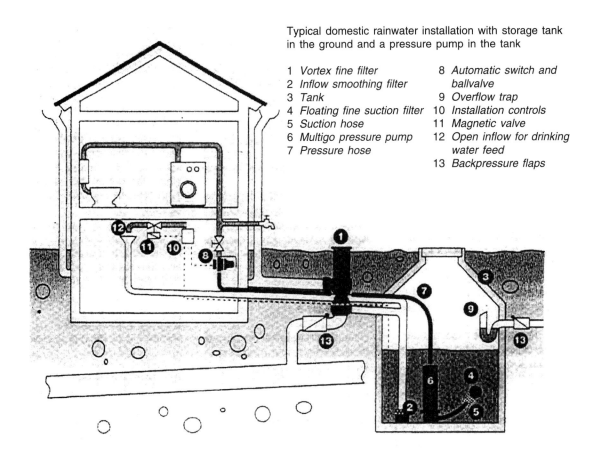

Typical domestic rainwater installation with storage tank in the ground and a pressure pump in the tank

1 *Vortex fine filter*
2 *Inflow smoothing filter*
3 *Tank*
4 *Floating fine suction filter*
5 *Suction hose*
6 *Multigo pressure pump*
7 *Pressure hose*

8 *Automatic switch and ballvalve*
9 *Overflow trap*
10 *Installation controls*
11 *Magnetic valve*
12 *Open inflow for drinking water feed*
13 *Backpressure flaps*

Figure 11.1
Rainwater storage system layout. Courtesy of Construction Resources.

purposes, other than drinking, it must be subject to further purification, usually by ultra-violet light. Best use of the filtered rainwater will be made if associated with dual flush WCs. Figure 11.1 shows a typical configuration for rainwater storage.

It is possible to go a stage further and use rainwater for drinking, but this requires even more rigorous filtration, as employed for example in the Southwell zero energy house designed by Robert and Brenda Vale and the Hockerton Project. In the former case the water from the roof passes through a sand filter in a conservatory. From here it is pumped to storage tanks in the loft and from there through a ceramic/carbon filter to the taps. As an act of faith in the English weather, there is no mains backup facility.

A variation on the water recycling strategy is to re-use grey water from wash basins, showers and baths. If waste water from a washing machine is included, then virtually all the waste water can be used to meet the needs of flushing toilets. Again there are systems on the market which serve this function, including water storage.

The Hockerton Housing Project has all these facilities and more because it uses rainwater collected from its conservatory roofs for drinking purposes. The water is stored in 25 000 litre underground tanks where particles have time to settle to the bottom. The water is treated first by passing it through a 5-micron filter to remove the remaining particles. Then it is sent through a carbon filter to remove dissolved chemicals. Lastly it is subjected to ultra-violet light to kill bacteria and viruses. The author can vouch for its purity! For the average home this may well be a step too far, but those who feel inspired by this possibility should contact the Hockerton Housing Project at www.hockerton.demon.co.uk

Rainwater recycling systems can be found at Construction Resources (Tel: 020 7450 2211; www.constructionresources.com).

For the really dedicated there is the composting toilet which eliminates the need for water and drainage. In Europe a popular version is the Clivus Multrum from Sweden. It is a two-storey appliance in that there has to be a composting chamber usually on the floor below the toilet basin. A fan-assisted ducted air ensures an odourless aerobic decomposition process. The by-product from the composting chamber is a rich fertilizer. A UK distributor is Kingsley Clivus Environmental Products Ltd, Winkleigh, Devon (Tel: 01837 83154; www.kingsleyplastics.co.uk).

For a comprehensive list of related products see: World of Composting Toilets (www.compostingtoilet.org).

Domestic appliances

As the building fabric of a home becomes more energy-efficient, the impact of appliances, such as white goods and TVs becomes a much more significant element of the energy bill. Refrigerators and freezers are particular culprits. In 1999 the European Commission decreed that all white goods, refrigerators, freezers, washing machines, dishwashers, etc., should be given an energy efficiency rating from A to G. This has certainly been effective in sending E, F and Gs to the bottom of the best buys. However, whilst A is the top of the scale, there is variation within this category and it is well worth investigating fridges and freezers which perform better than the threshold level for A rating.

Here are examples current at the time of writing. An example of an ultra-low energy chest freezer is the 'Norfrost 2000' which claims to be the 'world's most efficient freezer'. It has exceptionally low running costs at 20 p per week (at a unit rate of 7 p/kWh) which is a 65 per cent improvement over standard models. Over its lifetime it is reckoned to represent a cumulative saving of 75 per cent as against the norm. It is manufactured in Scotland (www.norfrost.co.uk).

There is also the Bosch 'Classic' range of refrigerators in the A category which use 212 kWh per year for an average household. This results in an approximate annual running cost of £14.84 (www.bosch-da.co.uk).

An organization which specializes in promoting super-energy efficient cold appliances is Energy+. The criterion for being included on its lists is that a product consumes no more than 42 per cent of the energy used by the average European cold appliance. It runs competitions and in 2001 the best two-door Energy+ fridge-freezer was the Electrolux ER8100B with an energy efficiency rating of 33 per cent against the norm.

The best one-door Energy+ fridge freezer was the Whirlpool ART 599/H with an energy efficiency index of 35 per cent (www.energy-plus.org).

Another manufacturer which is up with the brand leaders is Liebherr with its range of Class A fridges and freezers (www.lhg.liebherr.de).

The siting of a fridge-freezer can be important. For example, it should not be in the path of direct sunlight or near the cooker. It is important to ensure that door seals are fully functioning; inadequate sealing can result in a significant loss of efficiency. Also the temperature settings should be checked: 3 to 5°C for the fridge and −15 to −18°C for the freezer are the recommended temperatures. Fridge and freezer thermometers will prove a good investment.

Washing machines

The energy profile of washing machines has two aspects: the motor and the water heater. Most machines heat water internally by electricity and this may account for up to 90 per cent of the energy demand. If the domestic hot water system is heated by gas it would make sense to opt for a machine which draws its hot water externally. The ultimate energy efficiency is attained if it is supplied by solar thermal hot water. From an ethical standpoint *The Good Shopping Guide* (Ethical Marketing Group, London, 2002) recommends Candy, Hoover, LG and Miele.

Points to consider

- Front-loading machines are more economical in their use of water than top loaders.
- Machines which allow temperature and water level to be adjusted to the particular load are to be preferred.
- Most loads can be washed in warm or even cool water.
- Machines are most efficient when dealing with full loads.

Dishwashers

- As with washing machines, an appliance which uses water from a gas heated or solar thermal domestic cylinder is the most efficient.

- Where possible operate on short cycles.
- Ensure that the machine is loaded to capacity.

Finally, with all white goods it is vital to ensure that they are rated A on the EU energy efficiency scale. Where possible check the manufacturers' estimated annual energy consumption.

Stand-by consumption

A surprising amount of electricity demand is due to stand-by electrical consumption. Some appliances, such as televisions and personal computers, have optional standby modes which, nevertheless are left on power because the consumption involved is regarded as insignificant. Others, like fax machines and cordless telephones need to be permanently on standby. Even appliances with electronic clocks consume power. It has been estimated that a typical household could consume 600 kWh per year on standby alone. For the EU it has been calculated that standby power accounts for 100 billion kWh/year, about one-fifth the consumption of a state the size of Germany.

Main points

- Collect rainwater in water butts for irrigating the garden.
- Consider replacing fittings and appliances with water-saving features, e.g. spray taps and low flush or dual flush toilets.
- Rainwater collected from roofs can be collected and treated to be used to flush toilets and supply washing machines.
- More extensive treatment is required if roof rainwater is to be used for personal hygiene and even more for drinking.
- Composting toilets avoid the use of water and provide a useful source of fertilizer.
- When replacing white goods, only select appliances with an EU 'A' rating. Where possible select an appliance with an energy performance rating better than 'A'.
- If DHW is heated by gas, choose a washing machine which draws water from the DHW system rather than heating it internally by electricity.
- Avoid leaving TVs, PCs, etc., on standby. Standby mode wastes a considerable amount of electricity over time.
- When choosing a gas-fired central heating boiler, select a unit with electric ignition, rather than a pilot light.
- A useful source of information is *The Good Shopping Guide* which lays emphasis on the ethical aspect of choice (Ethical Marketing Group, London, 2002).

Materials

Chapter Twelve

Paints

Paints have three constituents: pigments for colour, a binding substance to hold the particles of pigment together and a solvent to enable the mixture to flow freely. It is the solvents which are the main problem since they are designed to evaporate. Most of the solvents used come into the category of volatile organic compounds (VOCs) and are aggressive pollutants. It has been calculated that over 500 000 tonnes of solvent are released into the atmosphere globally each year. (*Eco-Renovation*, Edward Harland, Chelsea Green Publishing Company, Vermont, USA, Revised edition 1999). Another statistic is that organic solvents are responsible for 20 per cent of the hydrocarbon pollution in the atmosphere and second only to motor vehicles (Berge, 2000).

It is the solvents deriving from the petrochemical industry which are the most toxic and which are implicated in the phenomenon of off-gasing. This may continue for a considerable time with sometimes serious health consequences. (A comprehensive list of surface treatments and their solvents is to be found in Berge, 2000: 405. Also refer to *The Natural Paint Book* (Edwards and Lawless, 2002) available from the AECB book service: www.aecb.net) There are alternatives, such as those containing natural resin emulsions. In their finish they appear much the same as conventional petrochemical emulsions and are as easy to apply. They are solvent-free and do not have the pervasive smell of chemically based paints. They are also biodegradable. An example for interior walls is Aquamarijn Maril matt emulsion class 2.

A traditional paint system for walls and ceilings is one which is supplied in powder form to which water is added just before use. It is made from natural substances and comes in a variety of colours. It contains no harmful chemicals and is washable after curing. A proprietary brand is Holzweg Cassein wall paint. The Holzweg colour range includes 21 natural earth pigments and 15 mineral pigments.

Holzweg also produces benign paints for exterior use, as well as varnishes for timber and waxes for floor treatment. Exterior timber preservative paints come in Scandinavian Iron Oxide Red ideal for weather-boarding and garden timber. Aquamarijn Garol garden furniture oil class 1 is ideal for the treatment of exterior hardwood, penetrating the timber protecting it from weathering.

All the above products are available from Construction Resources Ecological Building Supplies, 16 Great Guildford Street, London SE1 0HS, Tel: 0207 450 2211, e-mail: info@ecoconstruct.com

A natural paint collection is available from The Green Building Store. Its emulsion paints Primasol and Ecosol are solvent-free. Ingredients include chalk, linseed oil, talcum, earths and bergamot oil (www.greenbuildingstore.co.uk).

Natural Building Technologies uses paint formulae with ancient origins. Its range includes Scandinavian Red Paint, a water-based timber preservative using only natural materials. Information from www.oldhousestore.co.uk

Auro Organic Paint Supplies offers water-based gloss and eggshell paint finishes which avoid VOCs, They are quick drying and can be thinned with water (www.auroorganic.co.uk).

Ecosil from Keim is also VOC-free. It is alkaline and totally inert and prevents algae and mould growth without the use of plasticizers and biocides. It is durable and easy to clean. Its water-solvent, interior, silicate-based paints use organic fillers and pigments (www.spec-net.com.au/company/keim.html).

Nutshell Natural Paints are derived from natural materials, such as plant oils and minerals. Its interior emulsion includes linseed oil and beeswax (www.nutshellpaints.com).

Other ecological paints products are:

- Livos natural paints
- Casa paints
- Ecos organic paints from Lakeland Paints Ltd
- Solvent-free paint strippers include 'Homestrip' and 'Eco-Solutions'.

Many of these products can be obtained from Green Choices DIY section (www.greenchoices.org). Some of these products may also be found in Homebase and B&Q stores. Further advice can be obtained from the Ecological Design Association, www.edaweb.org.

Humidity

The choice of paints and varnishes can have an impact on the level of humidity within the home. Temperature is the key factor in determining how much moisture the air can hold. At 20°C air can hold 14.8 g/m^3; at 0°C it can only hold 3.8 g/m^3. On average, a living room contains 5–10 g/m^3. Fluctuations in temperature will alter the carrying capacity of the air and may result in condensation. It is important that the materials of the walls can absorb much of this moisture which means the use of hygroscopic materials, that is, materials that can take up moisture. Such materials act as a stabilizing agent, keeping the humidity level reasonably constant. In other words, hygroscopic materials have a damping effect on moisture fluctuations just as thermal mass regulates temperature (Berge, 2000: 251–253).

It is recommended that internal walls should be finished in hygroscopic emulsion paint over plaster. This ensures that excess moisture can be absorbed by the plaster and masonry wall, releasing it when the internal humidity level creates imbalance. A further benefit is that water vapour carries some gas contaminants, such as nitrogen oxide and formaldehydes. When the water vapour enters the hygroscopic materials these chemicals may be deposited and broken down giving these materials a degree of air cleansing capacity. However, the transfer of moisture will not happen if wall surfaces have impermeable finishes, such as oil-based paints or varnishes, plastic wallpaper or even wallpaper fixed with plastic-based pastes. Internal walls need to breathe, otherwise condensation is virtually inevitable.

Materials for the near future

Saving energy is one thing, buildings as carbon sinks is another. Yet this is the destiny of buildings according to John Harrison, a technologist from Hobart, Tasmania. He has produced a magnesium carbonate-based 'eco-cement'. In the first place it only uses half the energy for process heating required by calcium carbonate (Portland) cement. The roasting process produces CO_2 but most of this is reabsorbed by a process of carbonation as the cement hardens. Using eco-cement for such items as concrete blocks means that nearly all the material will eventually carbonate resulting in an absorption rate of 0.4 tonnes of CO_2 for every tonne of concrete. The ultimate eco-credential of this material is the rate of carbon sequestration. According to Harrison, 'The opportunities to use carbonation processes to sequester carbon from the air are just huge. It can take conventional cements centuries or even millennia to absorb as much as eco-cements can absorb in months', ('Green Foundations', *New Scientist* 13 July 2002: 40). This means that an eco-concrete tower block can perform the same function as growing trees as it steadily fixes carbon. Harrison estimates that a shift to eco-cement could ultimately cut CO_2 emissions by over one billion tonnes, since it could replace 80 per cent of uses currently served by Portland cement.

There is one further attribute to this material. Being less alkaline than Portland cement it can incorporate up to four times more waste in the mix than conventional cement to provide bulk without losing strength. This could include organic waste which would otherwise be burnt or added to landfill, sawdust, plastics, rubber and fly ash.

Eco-cement is not unique in its pollution absorbing properties. Mitsubishi is producing paving slabs coated with titanium dioxide which remove most pollutants from the air. In Japan, 50 towns are already using them and in Hong Kong it is estimated that they remove up to 90 per cent of the nitrogen oxides that create smog. Magnesium-based concrete coated with titanium dioxide could be the basis for eco-cities of the future.

Timber

A basic principle in using timber is to ensure it originates from a sustainable source, such as a managed forest. The problem is the degree of confidence one can place on a label. There have been numerous cases of timber being given this guarantee that have proved to be fraudulent. An inherent problem is that wood from, say, tropical rainforests, passes through any number of intermediaries before it gets to the UK market. At any one stage the authenticity of the sustainability mark can be compromised. There are reliable guides like *The Good Wood Guide* produced by Friends of the Earth or the National Green Specification (www.greenspec.org.uk). Similarly, *Construction Resources* is a reliable guide to ecologically reliable timber.

The officially recognized certification scheme for sustainably managed timber is operated by the Forest Stewardship Council (FSC). The council runs a global forestry certification scheme based on two key principles: forest management and chain of custody certification. The FSC label is claimed to indicate that the wood comes from a well-managed forest/wood and guarantees that its place of origin has been independently verified.

In the UK over one million hectares of forest and woodland are FSC certified which represents 38 per cent of total forest cover. Some certificates cover groups of woodland under single management, such as the UK Woodland Trust. Certification covers European and North American hardwoods and softwoods and certain tropical hardwoods. Unfortunately, there have been questions raised about the efficacy of FSC certification in South East Asia in a report by the UK-based Rainforest Foundation *Trading in Credibility* (November 2002) which states, 'The public cannot be assured that wood products carrying the FSC logo comes from a well-managed forest'. It cites numerous instances of certification granted in doubtful circumstances. Nevertheless if the FSC as the internationally recognized body with a certification scheme takes account of the criticism levelled against it, confidence should be restored (www.fsc-uk.info).

There is a wide range of temperate hardwoods which are an alternative to the tropical variety. Native hardwoods tend to have greater resistance to weathering and pests than the tropical varieties.

Examples are oak, beech, ash, elm, birch and sycamore. Their sustainability credentials are also usually impeccable. The UK has embarked on an ambitious reforestation programme with a mix of deciduous and coniferous trees. Pine is a good all-purpose softwood available in large quantities from managed forests.

In replacing timber doors and windows, the two things to remember are:

- Ensure that they have FSC certification, preferably from a temperate source. DIY stores are not always all that discriminating.
- They conform to the current building regulations.

The same applies to windows where timber is the ecological material of choice, rather than products from the petro-chemical industry.

Finally, with all materials, there is a degree of embodied energy, that is, energy expended in the processes of production and transportation. This is a huge subject which is being tackled by the Building Research Establishment. However, it certainly helps to use materials that are from a nearby source and therefore have the minimum of so-called carbon miles. As another example of reducing the ecological impact of production and transport, architects Robert and Brenda Vale used bricks from a local works fired by methane from a landfill site for their zero energy house in Southwell, Nottinghamshire.

Main points

- Paints and varnishes should be free from volatile organic compounds.
- Various brands of water-based paints are suitable for both internal and external use.
- For internal walls emulsion paints with hygroscopic characteristics reduces condensation.
- Wood should be certified by the Forest Stewardship Council as coming from a sustainable source.
- Timber from such a source is the ecological choice for window frames.

Chapter Thirteen Waste disposal and recycling

'The Earth is infinitely bountiful', so say the eco-sceptics. The reality is that society cannot continue to consume natural assets at the current rate. For example, the ecological footprint is the area of land (and sea) taken up to meet the needs of individuals or societies. A citizen of the USA uses 34 acres; in the UK the average per capita is 14 acres; Pakistan, 1.6 acres. Worldwide the average is 4.5 acres due mainly to consumption in the industrialized nations. In ecological terms this means that the Earth is already living beyond its means. For example, in 1962 it took 0.7 years for the annual biological harvest to regenerate. Currently it takes 1.25 years which means the natural capital account is going increasingly 'into the red' (Wackernagel, 2003). This provides the context for considering the problems of waste.

The waste being generated by the increasing consumerist ethos of the industrialized nations imposes four penalties:

- Depletion of natural resources;
- Energy involved in disposal;
- Increasing pressure on land for waste disposal;
- Pollution arising from landfill disposal.

There is a temptation to think that when waste is thrown away, that's the end of it. Far from it. From being our problem it becomes someone else's. At the same time we may be placing a valuable recyclable resource beyond use. As the natural capital of the Earth is being steadily eroded this is increasingly an ethical, as well as an economic problem. Land is Earth's most valuable commodity which is being increasingly diminished by building development and landfill sites.

The trouble is that society is schizophrenic. On the one hand the market economy encourages evermore vigorous consumerism which, in turn, increases the rate of obsolescence. Packaging and style upgrades exploit the human drive to be seen to be in the height of fashion. The irony is that our most expensive artefact after a house is the car which is designed for increasingly longer life. More and more cars are being claimed to have passed the million mile mark. So, constant style changes and technological tinkering, rather than functional efficiency, are needed to keep the market buoyant. Nations measure their success by the level of per capita GDP and the extent of annual economic growth. These dictate a nation's standing in relation to other countries, not least within highly influential bodies like the International Monetary Fund and World Bank.

The consequence of this is that there is growing concern about how to dispose of the escalating quantities of waste. The solution starts in the home. Local councils are under growing pressure to collect waste in segregated bins to facilitate recycling. This should be a major issue in local elections. At the same time householders can do a great deal to help the process along by:

- Re-using items wherever possible, notably plastic bags and containers.
- Composting organic kitchen waste and most garden waste (some plants are not suitable for composting). Some councils offer composting bins at a discount.
- Separating waste at source and, where there are not segregated collection facilities, delivering to appropriate waste bins.

There may be an added incentive to reduce the amounts of household waste. Plans are being considered to levy a charge for each bin collection from a home.

Recycling

We are slowly moving to a position where there will be no such thing as waste, merely transformation. This is what recycling is mainly about.

It is in the sphere of building that recycling has considerable potential, and this applies to renovation as well as new build. There are at least three aspects to this:

- Re-used items for the same or an alternative purpose;
- Refurbished materials;
- Reconstituted materials.

Re-use

Building demolition provides an endless source of items which can be re-used with almost no adaptation. Architectural salvage has become a significant industry. A first point of reference could be The Architectural Salvage Index operated by Hutton and Rostron (www.handr.co.uk/salvage_home.html; E-mail debi@handr.co.uk; Tel: 01483 203221). This index was started in 1977 to recycle building materials and architectural features from buildings which are being demolished or renovated. The index covers

- Building materials: bricks, slates, tiles, stone and timber
- Internal features: panelling, flooring, fireplaces, stairs, windows, doors and central heating items
- External features: a range of garden features and furniture
- Complete structures: barns, conservatories and pergolas.

There is also N1 Architectural Salvage at www.salvoweb.com/dealers/n1architectural for architectural features and www.salvoweb.com/dealers/v-and-v/index.html for reclaimed bricks, flagstones and other heavy items.

Refurbished materials

As the pace of economic change accelerates, relatively recent buildings are being demolished to make way for more intensive and lucrative site development. This means that many items are being dismantled long before they should be retired offering good opportunities for refurbishment. Radiators, pumps, etc., are obvious candidates. An example of the re-use of radiators from a demolished building is the Conference Centre at the Earth Centre, Doncaster, designed by Bill Dunster Architects (Smith, 2001).

Reconstituted materials

In refurbishment schemes it is likely that there will be some element requiring the use of concrete. This is normally an energy-intensive material due to the mining of aggregate and the production of cement. Normal concrete uses about 323 kg/m^3 of cement. This figure can be substantially reduced by the introduction of ground granulated blast furnace slag (GGBS) to provide additional bulk. This can reduce the cement content by 70 per cent in mass concrete for bases, etc. The only drawback is that the curing time is increased from the normal 28 days to 56 days. In many situations this is not a problem.

The upgrading of the railways has resulted in a good supply of timber railway sleepers – an excellent source of recycled timber that can be put to a range of uses, particularly in gardens.

In the Earth Centre at Doncaster, timber supports for the main structure comprise recovered telegraph poles discovered accidentally in a lorry park!

Waste glass has found a new incarnation as decorative tiles and blocks. Crushed and mixed with resin, it is available in a wide variety of

Figure 13.1
Crystal Paving floors: A courtyard between flats in a housing development at Port Marine, Portishead, UK.

colours and textures. In translucent form it can be back-lit as illuminated flooring or walling (Figure 13.1). It is an ideal cladding material. (See Crystal Paving Ltd of Ecclesfield Sheffield, web address: www.crystal-paving.co.uk; E-mail info@crystalpaving.co.uk; Tel: 0870 770 6189).

The mountains of waste slate in North Wales are slowly being ground into powder form to be transformed into resin-based building materials which can receive a high polish. As wall tiles they have the appearance of polished granite at a fraction of the cost.

In Chapter 2, there was reference to cellulose-based insulation derived from newsprint. It is particularly appropriate for loft insulation. Warmcel-RF is produced by Excel Fibre Technology, Ebbw Vale (www.house-builder.co.uk).

Further sources of information

National Recycling Forum (UK), *Buy Recycled Database and Guide* (www.nrf.org.uk/buy-recycled/index.html). This is a regularly updated database of recycled-content products and materials. It provides details of over 1000 products available in the UK. For each of the products the database provides information on:

- Type of reclaimed material in the product, e.g. paper, metal, etc.
- Percentage of post-consumer waste
- Percentage of other recovered material, e.g. production scrap

- Brand names
- Details of suppliers, including minimum amount which can be supplied
- Other technical information.

 Waste and Resources Action Programme (UK) (WRAP), *Recycled Materials and Products Information Portal* (www.wrap.org.uk). WRAP aims to find the best available information on UK reprocessors and processors of recycled materials. It offers to provide the best information and guidance sources on where to buy recycled products and materials.

 Construction Industry Research and Information Association (UK) (CIRIA), *The Reclaimed and Recycled Construction Materials Handbook* (www.ciria.org.uk). The handbook provides guidance and information on using reclaimed and recycled materials. It is wide in its scope and is aimed primarily at architects, builders and clients.

 Faber Maunsell's Sustainable Development Group and Ecological Development (UK), *Ecoconstruction Database* (www.ecoconstruction.org). The site contains guidance on choosing and specifying recycled products and materials, including those relevant to home owners. The site is sponsored by the Housing Corporation and SITA, and offers product search categories, rating method and case studies. There is information on:

- Recycled materials used in a product
- The manufacturing process including any use of toxic materials
- The capacity of the product to be recycled in the pre- and post-consumer stages
- Emissions during manufacture
- Percentage recycled content
- Place of manufacture.

The database has a significant number of products with a recycled content of between 80 and 100 per cent.

As EU regulations regarding the disposal of waste and the recycling of materials become more stringent, it will become increasingly economical, as well as ethical, to make maximum use of recycled and reconstituted materials. There is growing awareness that the Earth has a strictly limited carrying capacity and humans have already exceeded the power of the Earth to regenerate in many areas.

Main points

- Re-use items wherever possible.
- Compost organic kitchen waste.

- If there is no local collection facility for separated waste, deliver to appropriate collection points.
- Where possible use materials which have been recycled, refurbished or reconstituted.
- Ensure that waste from any refurbishment building work is minimized.
- Such waste as there is should be recycled or reconstituted wherever possible.

Note

Reference to any product, manufacturer or website throughout the book does not imply endorsement by the author. The author and publishers cannot accept responsibility for the performance of any of the products described. Similarly every effort has been made to ensure the accuracy of information. However, the author and the publishers cannot accept responsibility for errors and inaccuracies which may occur.

Chapter Fourteen   The wider context

This book has offered prescriptions for change at the level of the individual home. To end, the argument for change should be reinforced by placing it in its wider context. It may seem there is a wide gulf between the actions of a single home owner and the geopolitical forces that are shaping up for a contest in the global arena. The reality is that it is people that have the critical mass to shape the destiny of nations and corporations if they choose to exercise their influence.

It has to be accepted that the payback time for some of the measures described here is quite long. Payback time is the period it takes to recover the cost of the installations in terms of energy saved. This is because fossil energy is artificially cheap due largely to the fact that it is subsidized to the tune of $300 billion a year. In addition, it is not penalized for the damage it inflicts on health, ecosystems and above all the atmosphere by driving climate change. The last is often referred to as the external costs. Thus, the cost-effectiveness of insulation and renewable energy are measured by making a direct comparison with delivered fossil energy saved or produced by the installations, ignoring subsidies and the external costs. There is hope that, in due course, the EU will rectify the anomaly of a system skewed so heavily in favour of the interests vested in the fossil fuel industries.

Large organizations like the fuel giants with their bureaucratic hierarchies, their heavy investment in plant and people and their commitment to a particular technology tend to resist a 'disruptive' technology, like renewable energy. They have an interest in maintaining the inequality of the status quo. They may invest in the occasional wind farm or produce PV cells, but their heart remains firmly committed to oil and why not since it is still highly profitable. Studies of technical innovation have shown that radical innovations have never been introduced by market leaders.

Even international treaties like the Kyoto Protocol are geared towards making the fossil fuel industries more efficient rather than replacing them with renewable energy. The Iraq war brings the protagonists into much sharper focus.

Being, for a moment, the devil's advocate: energy, as stated, is relatively cheap, still abundant and generally reliable, so why, at this stage, go to the trouble and expense of refurbishing our homes? As for the moral argument, yes climate change is now virtually an established fact, but for the UK the benefits might well outweigh the penalties. We may have to improve coastal defences and sacrifice some land to the sea, but that will be a small price to pay if Bournemouth comes to have the climate of Biarritz, as one member of Parliament put it. All manner of new flora and fauna will flourish in our Mediterranean climate.

The counter argument is that unless there are drastic CO_2 abatement strategies even the UK will not escape the fallout from climate change. For example, there will be the displacement of whole populations due to rising sea levels and crop failures arising from drought. Climate change refugees will be numbered in the millions placing enormous strains on northern Europe. The economic structures of the world will collapse and even the balmy UK will not be spared.

As briefly alluded to in Chapter 1, the UN Intergovernmental Panel on Climate Change (IPCC) Scientific Committee has asserted that, if CO_2 emissions are to stop increasing in the atmosphere, there must be at least a 60 per cent reduction in emissions of the gas by 2050, as against 1990 levels. To its credit the UK Government in its Energy White Paper of February 2003 accepts its obligation to achieve this goal. However, the latest information from the scientists at the Meteorological Office's Hadley Centre in the UK is that the rate of climate change is proving to be significantly greater than earlier predictions. One contributory factor is the prediction that the Amazon rainforest is likely to disappear within a few decades due to die-back caused by rising temperatures. This will release as much as 77 gigatonnes of carbon into the atmosphere, raising temperatures significantly above IPCC estimates. This means that CO_2 levels will rise well above the ceiling of 500 ppmv regarded by the IPCC as the safety limit (*New Scientist* 8 February 2003, p. 55). The only remedy is virtually to eliminate the use of fossil fuels in the developed countries in the shortest possible time. So, where do we stand at present?

In the industrialized countries the demand for electricity, mostly fossil generated, is rising inexorably due to a combination of accelerating urbanization and the proliferation of electrical devices coupled with increased spending power. According to the International Energy Agency (IEA), an arm of the OECD, the demand for energy rose 60 per cent between 1971 and 1990 within its member states. Its prediction for the period 1990–2010 is for a further increase of 48 per cent in consumption, based on a medium growth forecast. The IEA forecast shows that, by 2010, the OECD countries will have increased consumption by 77 per cent above the reference date of 1990. The IPCC assumed that if CO_2 emissions are stabilized at 60 per cent below 1990 levels by 2050 this would assume an increase in atmospheric concentrations of the gas from the present 380 parts per million by volume (ppmv) to 500 ppmv. There would be inevitable serious climate damage at this concentration. However, on present performance there would seem to be little chance of achieving the IPCC target by that date. It is more likely that we can expect CO_2 concentrations reaching 700–1000 ppmv with consequences that are unimaginable (*New Scientist*, op cit).

Unless something radical is done to overturn these IEA predictions on fossil energy expansion, the planet is in for an extremely bumpy ride a few decades from now. What are the chances? At the moment they seem slim.

Henry Ford emancipated Americans. Cheap personalized transport meant that urban populations would no longer be confined within compact cities. So the current tension within the Middle East is as much to do with town planning as military planning. The rapid growth of the US led to the exponential growth of its major cities – not in their down-town centres, but in the green and pleasant peripheries. Economically liberated millions opted to escape to the vast suburban hinterlands of Los Angeles, Dallas, Phoenix, Houston, etc., in endless low density developments which could only exist on the basis of private transport. When the author visited Albuquerque some years ago it had the same superficial area as Los Angeles with only a fraction of the population. The car is the machine which makes the US function. It is impossible for these places to be served economically by public transport. So, America is understandably locked in to an oil-based economy. Worldwide, motor vehicles account for about 33 per cent of oil consumption; in the US it is nearer 65 per cent.

The oil-based economy is a major component of corporate power which is increasingly controlling the destiny of nations through highly centralized networks of influence. Solar energy threatens the hegemony of this system, offering individuals release from the corporate grip. It raises the prospect of individual home owners becoming energy autonomous – a frightening prospect for the major oil and power generating companies who are mostly in denial about the prospects of a post fossil fuel world. Yet such a world is inevitable.

The US Geological Survey estimates that confirmed oil reserves amount to 118 billion tonnes. Even using the most optimistic estimate of reserves, these will be exhausted by 2035. Gas reserves are likely to disappear by 2040, though UK domestic reserves in the North Sea will have gone by about 2016. This leaves us with a relatively short time in which to replace an oil-based world economy with one centred on renewable energy.

The killer punch as perceived by the sceptics is that renewable energy sources could never fill the vacuum created by the demise of oil. Dr Hermann Scheer, a member of the German Parliament, challenges this view, using his own country as the example. Here the aggregate annual electricity demand is around 500 billion kWh. He calculates that if this were to be met by PVs alone it would require 5000 km^2 of solar panels. If mounted on walls and roofs of existing buildings, this target could be achieved using only 10 per cent of the building stock.

If wind power were to be the sole energy source, using the industry standard 1.5 MW turbine, that country would need 166,666 machines to be installed in areas with a sufficient wind regime (Scheer, 2002). Obviously neither is a realistic option on its own; a mix of renewable energy sources would be employed: burning of biomass produced by rapid rotation crops (zero net CO_2), biogas from the anaerobic digestion of waste, and wave and tidal power (Smith, 2002). In the UK, for example, a single tidal barrage in the estuary of the River Severn would provide 6 per cent of its electricity needs.

In the light of this analysis, it looks as though the initiative for driving down CO_2 emissions rests with the people rather than governments and multi-national corporations. Householders have a key role to play in this operation. They, more than any other group, hold it in their gift to achieve substantial abatement targets. Yet how can one householder be of any significance in the titanic battle which is emerging between energy ideologies?

The UK Government is coming to terms with the fact that the energy infrastructure will have to undergo radical change from a highly centralized to a dispersed or 'distributed' system. As Scheer puts it, 'The familiar pattern of centrally managed supplies of electricity, fuel, heat and process energy will be replaced by a comprehensive decentralized supply. The essential prerequisite for all this is the deployment of renewable energy, because only from renewable sources can energy be supplied overwhelmingly without long supply chains. Only then can decentralized technologies truly lead to a truly decentralized system' (op cit, p. 200).

What makes this a realistic option is the development of information technology (IT) which makes possible a system based on a proliferation of mini-grids. Communities may decide to collaborate to generate electricity from individual homes forming a local mini-grid, called 'islanding' in current government parlance. Information technology is now capable of managing the complexities of a system with any number of supply and delivery nodes without centralized control. It can deal efficiently with the interplay of supply and demand, providing hour by hour best outcomes for both suppliers and consumers.

This revolution in the realm of energy will be driven by a number of factors:

- The security factor. In the present international political climate the vulnerability of large power plants especially nuclear sites is a major concern.

- The inefficiency of long delivery chains with consequent line losses.
- The growing pressure to reduce CO_2 emissions and, at the very least, meet internationally agreed abatement commitments.
- The fact that the Middle East now controls the price and rate of production of oil creates uncertainties. Reducing reliance on areas of political instability is a high priority for the industrialized countries.
- The technological developments across the spectrum of renewable technologies.

Developing the last point, there is considerable research and development into more efficient and cost-effective low to zero carbon energy technologies.

There should soon be a quantum improvement in the cost-effectiveness of PVs even in the context of the extremely uneven playing field enjoyed by fossil fuels. Thin film technology on flexible substrates is well advanced; cells using a range of light-sensitive dyes are producing promising results with more exotic technologies on the horizon. PV cells which mimic photosynthesis are already in the laboratory: photoactive materials using photochemical processes.

Rapid improvements are promised in the efficiency and cost of fuel cells with the miniaturization of electrolysis units producing hydrogen feeding fuel cells suitable for a single dwelling or vehicle. We have noted how compact, high-performance Stirling engines are on the verge of being market-ready; work on heat pumps has the aim of raising their coefficient of performance (COP) to 8:1 (8 units of heat to 1 unit of electricity), which will make them significantly better than heating with fossil-based energy. Improved biomass and waste gasification technology will give additional impetus to the formation of community mini-grids.

The first priority outlined in this book has been the need to reduce the demand for energy. It is possible for householders to cut energy use by up to 60 per cent by employing measures described here. If, at the same time, a home can further reduce its demand for electricity by generating its own from PVs or wind etc., then the whole housing sector has the potential to head the march towards a near fossil-free future. If a 60 per cent demand reduction were spread across the housing sector in the UK it would result in a 12–15 per cent reduction in the nation's CO_2 emissions. The 2003 Energy White Paper recognizes that, as well as promoting renewable energy, there must also be government support for drastically reducing demand for electricity and gas. By the end of this decade, 90 per cent of gas in the UK will be imported, mostly from eastern Europe. At the same time, within about 15 years from 2003 all nuclear power stations will have been decommissioned.

The housing stock is the largest single cause of CO_2 emissions, larger even than industry or transport. To tackle the housing sector head on would be the most rapidly achievable and cost-effective way of reversing the present trend of year on year increase in emissions occurring in the UK. At the same time a national upgrading programme would create a new workforce. It has also been calculated that it would make a significant inroad into health service costs directly attributed to poor housing. (Goodacre *et al.*, 2002).

In conclusion, the first priority for home owners should be to reduce their reliance on energy. Good insulation coupled with efficient air tightness with heat recovery ventilation should reduce the heating requirement for the average home to a mere 1.5 kW – well under the rating of the smallest central heating boilers.

This book amounts to an invitation to householders to side with the ever-growing battalions who have opted to go with the flow of nature in their lives, drastically reducing their reliance on commodities that are threatening the planet and compromising the security of future generations.

Scheer signposts the way forward:

Global civilization can only escape the life-threatening fossil fuel resource trap if every effort is made to bring about an immediate transition to renewable and environmentally sustainable resources and thereby the end of the dependence on fossil fuels   (op cit, p. 7)

Appendix Case Study: Ecological refurbishment of a house in Oxford, UK

Osney Island is a quiet enclave Conservation Area in a corner of Oxford on the banks of the River Thames. A small, end of terrace house facing the river is a remarkable example of a comprehensive eco-upgrading of a 19th century property. Its owner, David Hammond, is an architect who has been committed to environmental concerns since before his graduation (Figure A.1).

Figure A.1
End of terrace house in Osney Island, Oxford, UK, showing the sun space created out of the side access passage. This will be the site for future photovoltaic cells.

Figure A.2
Ground floor showing dry lining during installation.

There follows a brief summary of the eco-refurbishment that has been carried out by David.

In the first place, the house has been comprehensively insulated internally. All directly exposed external walls have been battened out with between 75 mm and 125 mm Rockwool RWA 45 insulation, behind Fermacell dry lining (Figure A.2).

A rear timber frame extension has been added, insulated with 100 mm of Rockwool between the framing and 50 mm Kingspan insulation across the framing internally. The loft space has been utilized as bedrooms with insulation following the profile of the roof.

The second major feature of the refurbishment process is the production of solar thermal energy via flat bed solar collectors.

The south-facing roof of the ground floor extension is devoted to supporting five solar panels: 7.5 m^2 Viessmann flat bed collectors (Figure A.3). These contribute hot water, at temperatures up to 65° C, serving the underfloor heating of three floors.

The hot water is directed to a 200 litre insulated cylinder (Figure A.4) which serves both the space heating and domestic hot water demand. There is also an immersion heater which, so far, has not been needed.

The heat pump installation was referred to in Chapter 7 (see section on the installation p. 51). It is a 6 kW unit provided by Kensa Engineering of Falmouth, UK. This is a breakthrough since it extracts heat from the River Thames. Anyone wishing to follow this precedent must have determination and patience to navigate through all the permissions and licences necessary which, in this case, involved:

Figure A.3
Viessmann solar thermal flat
bed collectors.

	Cost
Environment Agency abstraction application	£110
Annual Environment Agency abstraction/discharge fee	£25
Oxfordshire County Council Section 50 license	£600
Environment Agency mandatory water vole survey	£33.71

The heat pump is set to produce heat to a limit of 40°C which is its peak efficiency temperature. This is an acceptable temperature for most domestic hot water purposes. The hot water system is prioritized in favour of the solar collectors. The heat pump cuts in when the solar thermal water temperature falls below 40°C, and as a result, the heat pump is predominantly for winter use.

Space heating is topped up, if necessary, by an open fire with a controlled vent and flue baffle which cuts out heat loss when the fire is not functioning (ref. Chapter 5, paragraph 1). It is only needed on extremely cold days.

The next stage in the upgrading process is to install PV panels on the sun space, taking advantage of current government subsidies.

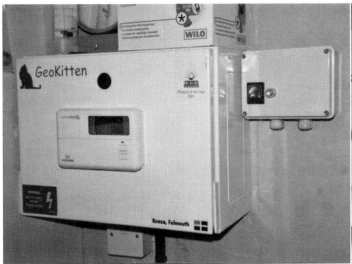

Figure A.4
GeoKitten water flow temperature monitor and 200 litre cylinder.

Systems such as this need time to bed in and there is continual monitoring to fine tune the system.

As this is a three storey house with an open plan ground floor, a safety measure, a domestic 'misting' type sprinkler system, has been installed.

Finally, the most ambitious plan of all is to develop a community-based micro-hydro installation at a nearby lock on the river. A weir at the lock provides a 2 m fall which is considered to be the minimum head of water for a viable micro-hydro project. If successful, this could set a pattern for numerous community schemes, both for navigable and non-navigable waterways. In the latter case a weir would be necessary to provide the head of water.

The benefits of the system, as described by the owner, are:

- its operation fully measures up to expectations
- it helps to reduce CO_2 emissions
- space heating and domestic hot water bills have been reduced by at least half
- it creates a 'pleasant thermal environment without radiators'.

Suppliers	Cost
Viessmann solar panels Contact: Hugh Jones Tel: 01952 675000 e-mail: info-uk@Viessmann.com Installation by LS Services of Bath	£3665 + 5% VAT
GeoKitten 6 kWh heat pump Kensa Engineering Contact Richard Freeborn Kensa Engineering Tregoniggie Industrial Estate Falmouth Cornwall e-mail Richard@kensaengineering.com	£3095 + 5% VAT including circulation pump, piping, filtration and casings
One metre deep trench from river to house by specialist subcontractor	£1500 including insurance required by local authority
Also Geoscience Ltd, Falmouth Contact Dr Robin Curtis Web site www.geoscience.co.uk	
200 litre insulated water cylinder and controls	£1300

The main contractor was Wooldridge and Simpson, Oxford.

Units of measurement of electricity and energy

Watt	basic SI (international system) measure of electricity (1 joule/second)
joule	basic SI unit of work or energy
kW	1000 Watts
kWh	kilowatt hours (kilowatts of electricity consumed over 1 hour)
kWh/y	kilowatt hours per year
MW	megawatts: 1 million Watts
GW	gigawatts: 10^9 Watts (one thousand million Watts)
terawatts	10^{12} Watts (one million million Watts)
petajoules	10^{15} joules (one thousand million million joules)

References

Berge, B. (2000) *Ecology of Building Materials*. Oxford, Architectural Press.

DETR (1999) Fuel Poverty; The New HEES.

Construction Resources

Earthscan (2002) *The Solar Economy*. p. 64.

Edwards, L., Lawless, J. (2002) *The Natural Paint Book*. AECB.

Energy, The Changing Climate, (2000) 22nd report, p. 169.

Goodacre, C., Sharples, S., Smith, P.F. (2002) Integrating energy efficiency with the social agenda in sustainability. *Energy and Buildings* 34:53–61.

Intergovernmental Panel on Climate Change (IPCC) (2002) Third Assessment Report.

Liddell, H., Grant, N. (2002–3) Building for a future, Winter, Eco-minimalism, p. 12.

New Scientist (2002) 173, 2332.

New Scientist (2002) 13 July 2002, 40.

New Scientist (2003) 8 February 2003, 55.

New Scientist (2003) 25 February 2003, 19.

Rainforest Foundation (2002) *Trading in Credibility*.

Scheer p. 7. (2002) *The Solar Economy*. Earthscan, London.

Smith, P.F. (2001) *Architecture in a Climate of Change*. Oxford, Architectural Press.

Smith, P.F. (2002) *Sustainability at the Cutting Edge*. Oxford, Architectural Press, pp. 53–62.

Thomas, R. (1996) *Environmental Design*. E&FN Spon, p. 10.

Wackernagel, M. (2003) Redefining progress. *The Guardian* 20 February 2003.

Washington Worldwatch Institute (2003).

Index